To Kirk & Annalisse,

St [on] Vacation

In the middle of a pandemic
A Memoir
Revised

Enjoy!
Love,
Ilean

Ilean Baltodano

From my childhood to my three-week vacation in USA

Contents

By day, the Lord went ahead of them in a
pillar of cloud to guide them on their way
And by night, in a pillar of fire
to give them light, so they could
travel by day or night.

—Exodus 13:21

Foreword

We have known Ilean since the early 1970s when she and my husband worked for Exxon in Nicaragua. Since reconnecting after both our families went into exile in the USA during the 1979 revolution, Ilean has been a wonderful friend and important donor and advocate for the Asociación Pan y Amor mission in Nicaragua. Pan y Amor is a mission offering an excellent education to children from some of the poorest and most urban neighborhoods of Managua, Nicaragua. Ilean's memoir reflects her journey, determination, and spirit that she now gives back to the children of Nicaragua.

Charlotte Somarriba
President, Asociación Pan y Amor
Managua, Nicaragua

Ilean's Memoir is the story of a truly remarkable woman who can do anything. In the course of her life, she has faced challenges that would bring most people to a complete halt. Not Ilean. She epitomized the belief that determination, focus, and unrelenting hard work can conquer any problem. And she was right. She met the challenges of an immigrant family, of integrating into a large corporate environment, of advancing her education, and of being widowed and raising her five girls. And she never stopped being the person that everyone around her cherished and loved. Ilean can do anything.

John F. Hughes.
Ilean's supervisor at Chevron and good friend ever since.
San Francisco, California

I have always admired Ilean for her tenacity, grace, intelligence, and incredible positive energy. She and her family are very special to me, a rare friendship and a family connection that has endured across generations and continents.

I've known Ilean since before either of us can remember; our parents were neighbors and close friends in Nicaragua. We had a very close bond with her. I remember Ilean used to style my hair as we sat outside in the small garden in her backyard, or how she would take me to visit her favorite places.

Later, in high school, she met Francisco, her first boyfriend and later her husband. She was not allowed to visit him alone, so I was excited that she often chose me to accompany them. We would go to the movies, and Francisco would make sure to get me popcorn and soda—rare treats at that time in Nicaragua.

When she and Francisco married, they created a successful life together. Later, when they needed to leave Nicaragua, they built their lives again in California with the same spirit and determination.

Her life is a remarkable example of the American dream. She, Francisco, and their young children immigrated to America with nothing aside from their extraordinary perseverance, tremendous work ethic, and Ilean's boundless positivity. True partners, Ilean and Francisco were devoted to each other and to their strong family unity.

She was always a good student—one who has never stopped learning. She led by example, showing her five daughters how to thrive in a professional career all while keeping family as the most important focus. From getting a university degree while working and raising her family to earning her master's degree, Ilean has always lived life to the fullest.

She has endless curiosity and an incredible love for life unlike anyone else I've ever met. I am grateful to be part of Ilean's life: first as children in Nicaragua and now here in California with children and grandchildren of our own. It is a gift that she has chosen to share her story with the world to be remembered for generations to come.

With love,
Ofelia Gallo
Modesto, California

Map of Nicaragua

Map of USA

United States of America

Prologue

Do one thing every day that scares you.
—Eleanor Roosevelt

It has taken me some time to process all the events in my life as a wife, as a mother, and as a citizen. Through this book, I will be sharing moments of happiness and moments of sadness in my life. This book will not change poverty, war, or hate. This book is not an analysis on immigration. This book speaks in the face of the struggle the United States is experiencing. Let's hope our children and grandchildren will change this beautiful and powerful country, which is not perfect but is great. Let's listen to each other: Asians, blacks, whites, and those with a Latino/Hispanic ethnic background. Let's not despair. Let's keep in mind, *"We the people."*

We are all different. Everyone is unique, although on a cosmic perspective as well as from a global angle, we are all the same. There is only one human race. We shouldn't be judged by the way we dress, the way we speak, and what we eat. Diversity is fantastic and should be celebrated. This is a memoir of experiences while unintendedly ended up on a long-term vacation in the United States of America. This story coincides with the immigration situation that is becoming inhuman to so many families trying to come to the United States. This topic is linked to the majority of Americans who are either immigrants, or descendants of immigrants. This book is quite simple but is for all of you.

The heroic immigration traffic into the United States of America is not new. It started with the first European settlement from around 1600. British and other Europeans settled primarily on the East Coast. Later, Africans were brought as slaves. The United States of

15

America has experienced waves of migration from all over the world. Initially and occasionally, it was acceptable but now is seen as a threat by some; hence, a restrictive and hostile environment causing chaos and despair to families. In reality, the decision to migrate to another country is a daring painful choice and a major risk.

Since the 1600, an immigrant's decision to move into the United States of America has been for safety, religious, and/or political freedom. This memoir portrays me as an immigrant who goes through fears and learning experiences. About an immigrant who travels to the United States of America for a three-week vacation but had to stay away from her beloved Nicaragua due to political reasons.

In 1979, I arrived to the United States of America, the land of milk and honey, with my family; and in 1980, I became a resident without any question, but that is not the case for everyone. In fact, as mentioned earlier, the terrible decision to leave your country is mainly for safety, religious, or political reasons, not whether you are legal or undocumented.

For me, as well as for the majority of immigrant's situation, the primary goal is safety. According to the Humanist Psychologist Abraham Maslow, our actions should be motivated primarily to achieve certain needs and safety, which are vital for survival.

Besides safety, you also look for acceptance into a foreign community, not just by your appearance but because you are a human being who should be treated with dignity and respect. Migrating is a journey full of bumps. My counsel is simple and straightforward: Don't give up and always keep up the faith and hope and be resilient. Believe in this country but also be aware that there is evil within it. There is so much hate, so much suffering, and so much insecurity everywhere, but harmony and love in our hearts is the prescription to this disease. Live every day as the present. Respect everyone regardless of their skin color, their belief, and/or any other differences. We all need love because it is part of our human nature.

It is sad to hear those who, because they are safe now, are shutting down the doors to others labeling all of them as criminals, or in the illegal drug business—not true. We cannot generalize. Their intolerance and arrogance are pervasive. It is so contradictory that there is so much hostility toward immigrants when the United States of America is a land of immigrants. The United States of America is a land that has historically welcomed those looking for freedom but now has changed.

This book is about a family struggling while looking for safety and freedom. So many families are currently persecuted or threatened by immature, neurotic, and unhealthy specimens with a cripple psychology and a cripple philosophy as Abraham Maslow would call them according to his Maslow's hierarchy of needs. Abraham Maslow developed the hierarchy of needs model in 1940s to 1950s in USA. The hierarchy of needs theory remains valid today for understanding human motivation and personal development.

It is indeed motivational how Abraham Maslow presents his theory in a pyramid illustration. This pyramid portrays how human beings have at the base of the pyramid, biological, and physiological needs such as air, food, drink, shelter, warmth, sleep, etc.

Maslow presents his theory as follows:

1. *Safety needs* (protection, security, stability, etc.)
2. *Belongingness and love need* (family, affection, relationships, etc.)
3. *Esteem needs* (achievement, status, responsibility, reputation, etc.)
4. *Self-actualization* (personal growth and fulfillment), which is at the top of the pyramid.

I see how, as an immigrant, the individual is primarily looking for safety and/or freedom no matter what the law indicates.

I currently live in California, and the following resounded in my heart: *In California, even though we don't have a Statue of Liberty, we have the Golden Gate Bridge. In California, we don't build walls, we build bridges.*

Thank God there was no wall when our initial settlers came to this country. I wonder if under this current atmosphere they are frowning.

To Those Looking for Safety
Ilean Baltodano

Are you looking for safety?
As I did once
Are you scared?
As I was once
What is your name?
Alien? Illegal?
Dreamer? Deportee? Undocumented?
These are not your names
You have a name
Courageous!
There are no walls
While looking for safety
While looking for shelter
Rules and laws have no meaning
Immigration laws are causing a ripple effect
We are all in the same boat
If the boat sinks
We all sink

CHAPTER 1

Timely Vacation

Laughter is an instant vacation.
—Milton Berle

Beginning back in 1978, there was a growing political unrest of the current Somoza Dictatorship and government in Nicaragua. For the past couple of years, there had been resistance and protest opposing the government, and as a result, there had been a higher military presence in the streets.

My husband, Francisco, was a district attorney in Managua as well as handling other legal cases and workload as part of his own law office. He would handle legal work for the United States Embassy and so developed good working relationships with those that worked there. On Monday, May 28, 1979, one of his contacts from the embassy came to his office. The conversation soon turned to the subject of the current political situation in the country, and his colleague asked if we had any plans to take some vacation out of the country.

Francisco replied, "*Yes, we are going to California to visit Ilean's sister as we usually do every year around the middle of August.*"

His friend immediately replied, "*Francisco, I think that it would be in your best interest to leave with your family as soon as possible before the upcoming major national strike. You need to get your family out of the country for a while. Your daughters are too young, and the political situation in the country is uncertain.*" His friend went on to say that in the next week, on Monday, June 4, a major strike of the Commerce and Industry in Managua would begin.

A few weeks prior to the conversation between Francisco and his colleague, I had found an anonymous note that had been slid under our front door. The note read: *Watch out for your daughters!* When I read this note, I could feel my face turning red and panic rising up inside. In my haste, I immediately began tearing up the note, ripping it into tiny little pieces. I later regretted this reaction, but in the moment, tearing it up into tiny pieces meant that by destroying it, the threat would somehow disappear. I felt watched, and I felt like we were being hunted. Our family was likely a target because Francisco was the district attorney of Managua. This was considered to be a political position working under the current Somoza government. Therefore, if you were currently working for the government, it was presumed by those rebelling against the government that you were supporting the Somoza regime. So, although I can only speculate, this note was probably placed by the members of the revolutionary movement, the Sandinista National Liberation Front (FSLN).

Coupled with having received the note, Francisco's political position as district attorney, and the urgency of his colleague's suggestion to take the family out of the country for a while, we discussed taking our vacation sooner. We obviously became extremely worried, and yet at the same time, we were in a bit of denial of the seriousness, or even the possibility of an impending war. Fortunately, Francisco was a planning type, and a few things had happened recently that would be factors in our discussions. One of those factors was that he always made sure that our passports were up-to-date with USA visas. This only helped with eliminating a hurdle in our decision-making. It was Monday, and we had only a few days to decide whether to leave before the strike or until August as we previously planned. Finally, we decided to pack our bags and go on vacation in June instead of August.

Our red truck was packed and ready to go. Our two oldest daughters: Ilean, nine years old, and Claudia, seven years old, sat in the bed of the truck protected under the truck's camper shell. Our two younger daughters: Deborah, four years old, sat in the front of the truck in between Francisco and me, and Kattya, at only nine months old, sat on my lap. These were definitely the days before required car seats or seat belts. With everyone loaded in, Francisco started praying for safety on our journey, then he started the truck, and we began to drive away.

Annual vacations weren't anything out of the ordinary for our family. Francisco and I were two working adults with four daughters, and we worked hard and diligently. We saved money to provide for and enjoy our family life. For this vacation in the summer of 1979, we decided to drive, not to fly, from Nicaragua to the United States, crossing through Central America and Mexico and crossing the United States border into California to finally reach our destination in the Bay Area. This journey in a red truck would take us approximately four thousand miles away.

During the week in preparation for our trip and while Francisco was working, I was packing, cleaning, and organizing. While in this process, I came across some very important documents, which would later prove to be significant. I found Francisco's California driver's license and his USA residency document also known as the *green card*. I decided to pack these two essential documents and take them with us. Francisco's family had lived in the United States during his formative years approximately between the years 1955 and 1962. Francisco went to junior high and high school in the Bay Area, California.

With the hope of returning soon, we were leaving behind our house, family, friends, my parents, and siblings. We had left our home once before when the earthquake hit Managua in 1972. Now for the second time, we were leaving again and leaving behind everything. With some premonition that we made too quick of a decision and not knowing whether that decision was right or wrong, we were venturing off into what we believed would be a reprieve from the political unrest. Unsuspecting this would be a vacation that would last a lifetime, this three-week vacation has been a grand adventure.

With the new day comes new
strength and new thoughts.
—Eleanor Roosevelt

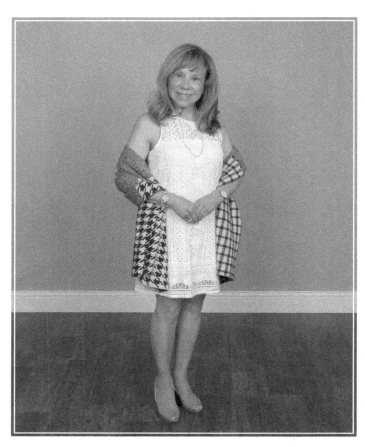

I am Ilean (IY-Liy-Ann)
April 2019

CHAPTER 2

I Am

To be or not to be that is the question.
—William Shakespeare
Hamlet

Who am I?

I am a child of the Most High, God. I am blessed. I have a fingerprint that nobody else has. My fingerprints are original. I am proud of the color of my skin.

I was born in Nicaragua. Managua is the land I grew up, went to school, worked for Esso, got married, started a family, and attended law school. Yes! That's me, Ilean.

Nicaragua is blessed with an abundance of natural resources and wonderful people. Managua is the capital of Nicaragua. *Managua* means "pouring water" because it is surrounded by water. Nicaragua is a small piece of land full of misfortunes either due to natural disasters or fighting among brothers. Nicaragua is described as the land of lakes and volcanoes, poetry, music, boxing, baseball, earthquakes, political instability, dictatorship from left and right, and the land of wealth and poverty. Internationally, many identify Nicaragua by the dictatorship of the Somoza family, or by the Sandinista revolution. The Sandinista government is currently a left-wing dictatorship causing pain and suffering to the country. Nicaragua is also known through the poet Ruben Dario who initiated the Spanish-American literary movement known as modernism.

My early childhood was formed through the influence of my father and mother and my older sister, Isabel, and the unique struggles of our family life. My father was an idealist and a writer, always hoping for peace and liberty through his beliefs in communism. In his ideal, he was fighting for justice, equality, and advocating for people that didn't have voices. However, looking back to the historical context of the 1940s and early 1950s, this was considered a radical position to take. Communism worldwide had been fought and conquered in places like Germany and Italy but still lived on in places like Cuba. My father would publish vignettes and poems of protest in local newspapers and work with local union syndicates expressing his dissent as to how the working class was oppressed and encouraging them to speak up. It was his communist philosophy and opinion that would eventually lead to his imprisonment when I was about five years old.

I was so young, but still I remember this horrible situation. My father was in trouble with the Somoza dictatorial government. On this particular early morning, I was awakened by a loud banging on our front door and a piercing shouting, "*Ricardo Zeledón. Police!*" It was a group of police officers that were searching for my father to arrest him. Immediately, my father leaps out of bed in a panic. He starts running through the house making his way to the backyard. He jumps over the fence to Dominga's house, our friend and neighbor. It is a fact, when you are looking for safety, you will jump any fence, any wall no matter how high it is, or whether it is built out of wood, cement, or steel. A fence or a wall will not stop you if you are looking for freedom, if you are looking for safety. My mother, in her nightgown, proceeded to opening the door. The police didn't say anything, just entered abruptly. Since my Dad had just jumped out of bed, he runs away barefoot and in his pajamas. Our neighbor, Dominga, sheltered him. She was able to find a suit, a hat, and shoes for my Dad and provided him with a few córdobas, which is the currency in Nicaragua. Now that he was ready wearing proper clothes, he left our neighbor's house through the front door. As he started walking casually and nonchalantly, he walked passed the police officers who were standing outside our front door. He walked next to them. While tipping his hat, he said, "*Con permiso*," which means, "*Excuse me*." He kept on walking without being arrested because he was not recognized.

He was able to find refuge at a Central American embassy in Managua. I believe it might have been the Costa Rica Embassy. I am not sure. I don't know the particulars or for how long he stayed at the embassy. For quite some time, he became a fugitive. The police kept looking for him, and after some time later while conducting a meeting with syndicate union working-class members, he was arrested. He was imprisoned for twelve long months. He mentioned two individuals who were in the same cell with him: Dr. Mario Flores Ortiz and Mr. Adolfo Baez Bone, who in 1954 was assassinated by the Somoza regime. The story as to how Baez Bone was assassinated by Somoza is terrifying. My father yearned to help the working class. In his declining years, he was disappointed with the Sandinista government. He no longer had energy to write poems. He was happy I fled to the United States, and before he passed away, he accepted the Lord as his savior. He passed away on December 14, 1997, at age eighty-eight.

It was at the time of his imprisonment that Mom became the most resourceful young mother to be able to raise and feed my sister, Isabel, and me. She was a housewife, or a stay-at-home Mom as they call them now, but through her ingenuity, she started going door to door literally knocking on doors and asking if they needed their hair done and styling women's hair as a hairdresser. She wasn't formally trained and never attended any type of beauty school, but through looking at magazines and imagination, she started styling women's hair using the latest hairstyles of the late-1940s/1950s era. Curls, smooth waves in the front, and rolled curls to the back as well as volume were the most used styles. If they had long hair, it was gathered in the back in a low bun. The rest of the hair was waved or curled on top of the head. She would wash, cut, and style their hair on a weekly basis.

It was one woman in particular that would prove to be a very important client. She purposely looked for this strategic contact. This lady was the wife of the person who was in charge of the political prisoners including my Dad. My Mom started a special connection with this lady. Consequently, my Mom obtained through this lady special permission to visit my Dad as well as being able to bring to my Dad homemade lunch. Soon enough, my mother started having so many regular clients that she was able to open a beauty salon, and she started working from home while Dad was still in prison.

While imprisoned, my Dad was living under unhealthy conditions. The sanction of political prisoners is totally indescribable. He was deprived of his liberty, no freedom of movement, no human rights, no self-esteem, and no dignity. Not even access to light and fresh air or exercise. He wasn't getting any sun, and due to the deprivation of sun exposure and malnutrition, his body was lacking vitamins and minerals. Four of his front bottom teeth became loose, and he eventually lost them. Sometime later while in prison, he was allowed to go out for a few minutes to the courtyard. The first time when he went to the courtyard, he saw the green grass and immediately threw himself down to the ground and started pulling and eating the grass, just like a cow, a horse, or a rabbit would do it. After a year, he was released, but because of his time in prison, he became extremely paranoid. He was afraid of individuals in military attire or uniforms, even afraid of traffic police officers.

During this time, my Mom would send me to stay with my godmother, Elena Arellano de Franceries also known as Nena. She lived near *La Chabela Lezama*, a popular corner store where you could buy milk and bread as well as alcoholic drinks. I would stay with her during the day while Dad was in prison, and so my Mom would be able to work and visit my Dad. My godmother's house was beautiful and neatly arranged. I always admired her collection of miniature *Limoges* from France, her piano, and the beautiful furniture and family pictures displayed around the house. The painful part while staying with her was in the afternoon when the Franceries would go to the country club and I had to go along with them. It was painful because I was attached to my Mom, and I was anxious waiting for her to pick me up even though my godmother's house was beautiful as well as going to the country club was a treat. It is so painful and detrimental when children are separated from their parents. I clearly remember this feeling. You want to be with your parents no matter what.

At the country club, the men would play golf with some of their friends. I still remember their last names: Najlis, Dreyfus, or Lichenstein. We, the kids, would play on the beautiful green grass and enjoy cold drinks. The place was beautiful and first class, but I wasn't interested because this was the time Mom would pick me up. I wanted to be with her, and I was ready to go home, not to the country club. I didn't care that the country club was beautiful; being with Mom and at my home was all I wanted. I remember my godmother Nena with so much respect and admiration. She was beautiful both spiritually and physically. Her mission was to help the leper's center. Every year, she would collect money through fund-raising as well as by placing wooden money boxes at large and small businesses, such as my mother's beauty salon.

It was an afternoon shortly after my Dad was out of prison when Mom went to buy groceries and provisions for dinner. She was going through the aisles and shelves and shopping when suddenly she was interrupted by a little boy who was selling his last two lottery tickets. *"Señora, please buy these two last lottery tickets from me. If I go home with them, my mama will spank me."* Since my Dad was right out of prison, he was having a really tough time getting a job, so for my Mom to spend money on buying lottery tickets was a major gamble, no pun intended, as this money needed to be spent on food. But still, the boy insistently kept begging her. Mom, a little bit uncertain, finally decided to buy one of the two tickets from him. She hid the ticket in her purse, bought the groceries, and went home. She didn't mention the lottery ticket.

The next morning, she checked the ticket. My Mom won the lottery! I don't know how much she won. I assume it was a good amount. My parents, already being very reserved, kept it a secret from friends and neighbors, so they invested most of the money in remodeling the beauty salon. They bought hair dryers, electric machine to curl the hair, manicure tables, pedicure/manicure utensils, shampoo chairs and bowls, Kelvinator refrigerator, and last but not least, the salon now had a name: *Isabilean*, the merging of my sister's and my name—Isabel and Ilean. They installed a large sign in the front with large glowing letters. The sign cheerfully illuminating the name throughout the neighborhood and we, all happy kids, played in the evening like fireflies under the light.

The beauty salon was a lot of work for Mom, but it was so much fun for me. It was so entertaining to be around the hairdressers always laughing, singing, or joking among them. I don't think they even realized I was around. I still remember the names of the hairdressers who worked for Mom throughout the years: Juanita, Lillian, Angela, Aurora, Argentina, Vilma, Myriam, and Silvia. While being around them, I could listen to their stories, which most of the time were jokes about some of the clients.

My father's imprisonment and the reason for his arrest were not a secret around the community. Some people looked down upon him especially given the reason for his imprisonment—that of a communist supporter. One day, as I was outside my house, an older lady started yelling and pointing at me, *"There goes the daughter of the communist!"* I didn't understand what this meant at the time, but hearing her yell and seeing her angry face, I knew her nasty tone of voice was directed at me. I felt attacked. I immediately went inside my house, and I mentioned this incident to my Mom. She said, *"Just ignore it,"* as if it would go away. But this occurrence did not go away throughout my childhood. Later as I grew up, I was able to figure out what being the daughter of a communist meant. The reality is that you don't pick your parents, or your family, or their ideologies. They are imposed on you. But as you grow up, you pick your own path, and the circle of life keeps moving generation after generation.

My father had an elegant writing style in which he expressed his thoughts and opinions in a poetic style, rhyming words, and manipulating the Spanish language. He was an excellent writer and public speaker. My father was a strong man, both physically and in the stubborn sense very dictatorial. He wasn't a sentimental type and even more so as we grew older, definitely no hugs or affection, but my father was a great storyteller.

As a very small child, I enjoyed falling asleep on his lap listening to stories or while he was reading the newspaper to Mom. His formal education did not include university level, but he was self-taught. He was an autodidact. My father was my first teacher. He taught me how to read and write at a very early age before even starting school. Rather than teaching me print style, he taught me cursive writing. To date, even though many people write print style, I have to make an effort because I will always prefer cursive. During my childhood, I would look at my father with a certain amount of fear because he was strict and severe with my mother, sister, and me.

I recall an evening when we had a scary thunderstorm with intense lightning. I was so frightened. The raindrops in tropical countries are thick and make a lot of noise on clay tile rooftops and even more on tin rooftops. Dad put it in simple plain words why I should not be fearful of lightning and thunderstorms. As some people would say, any time they would experience this type of storms, that *Papa Dios* was mad. *Dios* means "God." In fact, in some traditional religions and even some African tribes, lightning is a sign of the ire of the gods. My Dad took the time to describe the physical process of this electrostatic discharge that occurs during a thunderstorm. Thunder and lightning are a tremendous force of nature, which inspires to some fear and to others reverence, or fascination, as well as legends and religious representation. He would continue saying, "*Count the time between the bright lightning and the sound of rumbles, the loud crash. Thunderstorms are okay; they are just part of nature.*" He was trying to teach me to accept nature. As time went by, the sound of the thunder got weaker and weaker until it was gone along with my fears.

Mom was an incredible entrepreneur. My mother's beauty salon had a staff of four and up to six hairdressers during the holiday season. Her day would begin before sunrise as she busily prepared her business and would end late into the evening. She was a serene and gentle person and a dedicated mother and wife. Her positive, friendly, and jovial personality showed in her love to help people. Shortly after meeting her, you realized that you had met a special person. When I think about my mother, I remember her energy, strong work ethic, and resourcefulness that drove her entrepreneurial spirit. Her example greatly influenced my life and set the course for how I valued my work and life. She was born and raised in Nicaragua. Although I miss her laughter and the cherished time I spent with her, I am grateful that she died peacefully in her sleep. She passed away on April 19, 2017, at 10:30 a.m. On May 22, she would have turned ninety-seven years.

Eventually, my father was able to find a job as a life insurance salesperson. He did well. He was nominated many times as the number one salesperson of the year.

As a child, I had two pets: *Mascota,* my cat, and *Cosaco,* my dog. In English, these names mean *pet* and *Cossack*, respectively. I also had about ten chickens. They laid more eggs than we could use at home for cooking. It was at this point in my early life that I discovered that it was a good idea to start a business. I started selling eggs as well as baking cupcakes for the customers at my mother's beauty salon.

Many years later, we left that friendly neighborhood in which I had grown up, and we moved to a brand-new house away from downtown Managua, but still, we were able to stay in touch with most of our neighbors because the beauty salon stayed in the same area. Coincidentally around this same time, a bilingual American Catholic school was established in Managua. My mother said that the school was the answer to her prayers because it was an all-girl Catholic school and would allow us to learn English—*Colegio Teresiano*. I was also enrolled at the Alliance Française where I studied French. It was through my mother's vision that I was able to be exposed to the fundamentals of English. I also was exposed to French through the influence of my godmother, Elena Arellano de Franceries, who was married to a French Jewish, very gentle, short, quiet, and polite gentleman with a very cute French accent in Spanish, Raymundo Franceries; and their two children: Andres and Yvonne. I didn't see Andres very much because he attended a boarding school in Granada. I always looked forward to playing with Yvonne after she was back from school.

I was the youngest of two until many years later that my parents had three boys: Ricardo, Rolando, and Ivan. Isabel, my sister who is the oldest, is beautiful and smart. I depended on her so much when I was a kid. Even when I had issues or questions related to school, I would go to her because my mother was too busy at the beauty salon. I remember when I first had my menstrual period, I was so scared. I talked to her, and she was the one who explained the whole process.

When I graduated from high school, I prepared with the help of my sister to give the farewell speech in front of all the students at the graduation ceremony, and I was picked. But to my surprise, later, my teacher who was a nun, told me they had picked Irene because she had been one of the first students of the school when it was first founded. I started this school the following year. I went home crying and talked to Isabel. She had already graduated from high school, and she went to talk to Mother superior, Grace, and my teacher, Mother Maria de Los Angeles. They listened to her, and they were able to accommodate my request. Since the graduation ceremony was going to span two days, Irene would present the speech on the first day, and I would do it on the second day. When I did my speech, it evoked so much emotion that many of the students were teary. I did a good job because I did it coming from my heart. The speech was a poem I memorized from Saint Teresa of Avila entitled *Dulcisimo Recuerdo de mi Vida,* and the literal translation is *Sweet Memory of my Life.* In this beautiful poem, we were requesting God's blessing as we were departing school.

When I look back on my childhood, I have to be grateful for how blessed I was. I thank my parents for their perseverance and for their hard work. Even though I was born in modest circumstances,

I was raised in a good and safe environment. The Nicaragua I grew up was a diverse place that included descendants of immigrants: Jews from Poland, Jews from France, Germans, Arabs, Chinese, and European descents mixed with Nicaraguan natives.

I was raised in a neighborhood with kind and friendly people; although there were a couple of grumpy neighbors who didn't like noisy children. Just to mention some of the kids. Here you go: Laura, she was my role model; Yolanda; Isabel, my sister; Gloria; Armando, he loved Laura; Pedro, I was young, but I liked him; Luis, he loved my sister; Juan; Alejandro, he loved Yolanda and eventually married her; Alberto, he was a child with a physical impairment, but he was a sweet and happy boy; Silvia, Alberto's older sister; Felipe; Carlos, he married Gloria; Mario, his parents owned an ice cream business, *El Eskimo*; Hortensia; Maritza, Hortensia's sister; and Ofelia, Laura's sister. Ofelia was the youngest of all of them, and she is my close friend.

Going back to the neighborhood I grew up and the grouchy neighbors, they obviously didn't like any kind of disturbance, and all of us kids were running up and down the sidewalk most of the time. One time, this neighbor threw gravel on the sidewalk so that we would trip while roller skating, but that didn't stop us. Oh well, now I feel bad. Yes, we were too noisy. Sorry.

I'm still in close contact with some of the families who lived in the community of my childhood. In spite of all the time that has gone by, I remember most of the families. Some of the families that might not even remember me, I will always keep them in my mind and in my heart. Here is another list, this time, by last names: Carrasquilla, Salvo, Maltés, Mercado, Guerrero, Bermúdez, Pérez, Tellería, Sandino, Hubieta, Soto, Horvilleur, Suhr, Picasso, Toledo, Perez-Alonzo, Somoza-Medina, and of course, Tia Margot. She was a seamstress married to a well-known tall, friendly, and handsome attorney, Dr. Orion Carrasquilla, who came with his parents from Colombia. All the kids would call her Tia Margot except my sister Isabel and me; even though I wanted to call her Tia Margot, my Dad would say she wasn't our real aunt.

My nostalgias and recollections evoke the Managua before the Sandinista's regime took over and even better before the Managua earthquake of 1972. The Managua that I remember and that I am mentioning here is the Managua full of charm and memento that will never come back. The Managua, just as the Nicaraguan popular song goes, "*Managua, Nicaragua, where I fell in love.*" The Spanish title: *Managua, Nicaragua.* The American pianist, Irving Fields, composed this song, which was an international success. It was a hit by the RCA Victor Record winning first place in 1947 within the Anglo-Saxon world. Irving Fields was born in New York. He died in 2016 at age 101 in Manhattan, New York.

I remember the movie theaters close to the neighborhood, El Trébol and El Tropical. Later, more fancy theaters were built such as El Salazar, El González, and El Margot. Also, the ice-cream shop, El Esquimo, which was founded around 1942 as a small business and that eventually became a national ice-cream chain. Mario Salvo and his wife, Josefina Horvilleur, were the founders and owners. It was during the triumph of the Sandinista revolution in July of 1979, El Esquimo was expropriated by the Sandinista government. That is to say that many operations were seized and run by the Sandinistas. It returned to the Salvo family in the 1990s. There is a lot more about this, but that is another story. In 1992, Eskimo started expanding to the rest of Central America. I also remember the cement industry, *La Cementera*; the building named after President Somoza's daughter, Lillian, *La Casa Lillian*; the small cute Catholic church, El *Perpetuo Socorro* led by Father Corrales; the Chinese restaurant, Chop Suey, owned by a Chinese family born in Nicaragua. The sense of smell is so powerful, especially when you are young. How can I forget the little house that had a horrible disgusting smell because they fermented ripe plantain to distill vinegar? Just like apple cider vinegar, this was vinegar made out of ripe plantains.

For elementary school, I attended a private school: Colegio Renovación. It was located a block-and-a-half away from home. The owner and director of the school was a well-known and esteemed lady, Lucrecia Proveedor. Later when I started fifth grade, I attended the bilingual school: Colegio Teresiano. When I graduated from high school, I accepted a job with Esso through the recommendation of

Ana Maria Schutze, a good friend of my sister, Isabel, who both had already graduated from high school.

The job at Esso required some English knowledge, and I passed the test. The interview was short, and the test included typing a letter in English and Spanish. I got the job and was asked to report to work the next day. The dilemma was my father. He was extremely protective. He wanted me to stay home and to assist Mom at her beauty salon. I was so happy I had gotten a job with Esso. He wasn't happy. He forbade me to report to work the following day. After pleading and begging, he finally agreed but under one condition: I was to give my paycheck to my mother. That I didn't mind because I was not interested in money. I was proud and happy I had a job at a young age working for a big company.

I was fortunate working for a well-known company with great coworkers that I still remember, and I am still in contact with some. Initially, I was hired for three months, but later, they offered me a full-time job. I enjoyed working. A few months later, I was transferred from the Esso refinery to the main offices initially located in Managua, but later, we were moved into a new building across the refinery located at *La Cuesta del Plomo*. Working for Esso was interesting, stimulating and challenging. This was my first experience in the business world. It was exciting getting ready every morning just like when I was going to school but totally in a different environment.

Everything was great at Esso but not for very long. While working for Esso, I unfortunately ran into two depraves who tried to abuse me. The first incident happened while working at the refinery warehouse, and the second incident when I was transferred to the main office.

At the refinery warehouse, I was working for two men: A North American who was training the Nicaraguan supervisor. The three of us were in a small office with no big windows, just a tiny window at the top of the metal door heading to the warehouse. The warehouse was stocked with tools as well as Ingersoll Rand equipment for the refinery. The North American guy was a heavy smoker and would take frequent breaks to smoke outside the office. At the beginning, everything was moving on just fine. We all were doing what we had to do. To my shock, one morning when Mr. Goodman went out to take his break, the national supervisor got close to me and, without saying a word, got very intimate and started rubbing my right arm and my back. I jumped scared. I wasn't expecting this invasion. I was so young and naive. I was just out of high school. Any time Mr. Goodman would leave the office, the supervisor approached me and tried to touch me, and I would start fighting back. I was so terrified of him but kept quiet. I was embarrassed to mention it, and I was also hesitant to complain. I was fearful he would fire me for not letting him touch me. Then I decided that any time Mr. Goodman would go out, I would immediately follow him. I'm sure Mr. Goodman noticed my anxiety. I wonder why he didn't do anything. This was a frightening situation.

One morning, when the national supervisor happened to be out of the office, Mr. Goodman approached me quietly and mentioned that his contract with Esso was coming to an end. He mentioned he was leaving shortly, and he had requested the refinery manager to transfer me to the pool of secretaries located nearby the warehouse. I didn't say a word, but I was so happy. My anxieties and my fears were soon coming to an end. When the supervisor was informed that I was going to be moved out of the warehouse, he strongly argued that it was inconvenient for him to leave the warehouse every time he had to give me or pick up work, but the decision was made, and I was safe and away from this sexual abuser. I was so young, just out of high school.

A few years later when I was transferred to the main office, I also had an incident with one of the managers. He was one of the two sales managers. I had known him for quite some time, and I respected him. He seemed to be a good person. One day in December, he called me over the phone and asked me to come to see him in the afternoon before leaving the office because he had a present for me. December was the time Esso recognizes major customers with nice presents. I figured he was going to give me one of those leftover presents. I was getting ready to go home, the building was quiet, and I did as he asked me. I went to see him before leaving. He was waiting for me and greets me with a friendly smile. On his desk, I noticed a large present. It was covered with Christmas wrapping paper and a ribbon. I believe it was a glass punch bowl with cups. He stood up and gave me the box. The box was big, and I had to hold it with both hands. Of course, I was pleased. I didn't report to him. He was in the sales department. I was working for the operations manager. I looked at him and said thank you and of course ready to leave. I didn't come to socialize; just to get the present as he had mentioned over the phone.

As I was trying to leave his office, he grabbed me. I never guessed he had any bad intentions. I am a petite 5'2" and at that time about 105 pounds though short in stature with a lot of self-control. He was tall, strong, and heavyset. I dropped the big box and struggled for a few seconds. I was able to move fast and run away from him. My heart was racing, and I tried to calm down promising myself everything would be okay. I was so surprised he physically attempted to sexually abuse me. It hurt me very much. I didn't tell anybody about this incident. It was humiliating. It was embarrassing. It was offensive. It was invasive. It was sad. Why me?

I'm sure this scenario has happened to many young people, boys and girls. The reason I didn't mention anything to anybody was because I felt the company might not support me if I would come forward. That was my mistake, but I probably was wrong. I should have reported both of them. The head of the company was a person that to date I admire. I loved my job, and I felt complaining would have been suicide to me. I didn't want to sacrifice my job. It's hard when you are young. I just stayed away from these two guys. For quite some time, I had nightmares that the warehouse supervisor and the sales manager were coming to get me. When I was young, I was annoyed by my father's constant protection. I even thought he was paranoid, but now as a mother and as a grandmother, I agree with him. It is devastating to be a victim of sexual violence. There is a lot of pain as well as confusion when you have been sexually assaulted. Young people, boys and girls, unfortunately, monsters are everywhere. You have to be vigilant and suspicious with obsessive aggressors. Do not become a victim of sexual harassment. Sexual harassment is a criminal offense.

Later, I left Esso to attend law school at the Universidad Centro Americana (UCA) in Managua. Just two weeks after starting my fourth year of law, my studies were interrupted because of the political situation in 1979, which forced me and my family to leave Nicaragua.

When you reach the end of your rope,
tie a knot in it and hang on.
—Franklin D. Roosevelt

Love at First Sight!

CHAPTER 3

Meeting My Soul Mate

There are no accidental meetings between souls.
—Sheila Burke

It was truly love at first sight. I was a senior in high school when I met Francisco. From a distance, I saw a tall handsome young man walking in my direction. It would be the day that would change my life forever. My sister whispered to me, "*That guy coming toward us is Francisco.*" I said to myself, "*I will marry him.*"

I was still wearing the school uniform, and I was going to study with my friend Irene when I saw him again. I was getting ready to enter my friend's house located on the second floor of the NOMAR building, owned by her parents, when Francisco passed by in his yellow Ford car. I said again to myself, "*I will marry him.*"

Time went by, and approximately six to seven months later, he came to my house with his friend Franklin who was at the time dating my sister. Franklin was getting ready to move to California and came to say goodbye. He asked Francisco to join him so that Francisco would be with me while Franklin would be with my sister. I was so thrilled. Francisco was talkative, immensely charismatic, and of course, charming. He, too, was smitten with me. I didn't go after him. He came to me. He had moved back to Nicaragua from California with his family. Francisco's father, who was an attorney from Nicaragua while in USA, was an evangelical pastor and pastored a church in San Pablo, California. After several years of living in the United States, the Baltodano family moved back to Nicaragua, and I met my soul mate.

We started dating shortly after we formally met in my house and had a lot of fun together. We dated for six years before we got married. Francisco, as my boyfriend, was not accepted by my Dad. My Dad would constantly count the months and years we were courting. My Dad wanted a more traditional approach to our dating. He wanted Francisco to officially ask his permission to visit me and date me. On the other hand, I wasn't going to ask him to do it. We were so young and with so much ahead of us. My mother loved Francisco from the beginning, but of course, he knew how to charm her too. The relationship with my Mom was such that I didn't need to hide anything from her. I always told her what was going on. With my Dad, this wasn't the case.

At some point, to avoid my Dad's control, I decided to keep our dating a secret. The majority of the time we were dating, I was seeing him away from the house without letting Dad know.

After six years, we got married. Keep reading. I will continue sharing about our married life.

> *Love doesn't need to be perfect. It just needs to be true.*
> —Moora Rahat

CHAPTER 4

Powerful Earthquake

*In the center of a hurricane there is
absolute quiet and peace.
There is no safer place than in the
center of the will of God.*

—Corrie ten Boom

Why is it that when your life is moving on so well, all of a sudden something happens?

When we got married, Francisco and I were living with his parents. We were crowded into one big room, which included our bed, two night tables, a dresser, a crib for one-and-a-half-year-old Claudia and a twin bed for three-year-old Ilean. My husband was starting his career as an attorney with his Dad as his partner who was also an attorney. I was working for Esso.

Just before Christmas, on December 8, 1972, we excitedly moved into our new home. This was the ideal family Christmas present for my husband, our two daughters, and me. It was a spacious Spanish colonial-style home, which we had designed to fit our needs. Francisco's parents moved to live with us as well as his youngest sister, Maureen. The house was painted white and brown, with red-tiled roofs, high ceilings, five bedrooms, two living rooms, a formal dining room, a large kitchen, three-and-a-half bathrooms, a room for the housekeeper, and a three-car garage, which housed a white 1965 Mustang I had bought when I was single; a Ford car; a small red truck; a camping trailer; and last but not least, my husband's CBX1000 Honda motorcycle. The American dream is to own a house. It is also the Nicaraguan dream. At this time in our married life, I was more than overjoyed. Being accustomed to only a bedroom, this was luxurious and a dream come true.

The look of the house, the special scent of newness, the smell of new paint, the smell of wood, and the smell of wet soil in the front yard where a new lawn was being planted are all still vivid in my mind. Just like any new home, we had to buy a new refrigerator, pots, and pans. In other words, we were starting as newlyweds.

It was on the night of December 22, 1972, fifteen days after we had moved in, at about 7:00 p.m., we went for a casual walk around our new neighborhood. In only this short time, my outgoing and friendly husband knew almost everyone in the neighborhood, and they knew him. As we walked, we discussed buying our young two daughters a doll and some small trinkets for Christmas only three days away. There would not be many presents this year because of the one big present where we had invested so much money. We enjoyed seeing the houses with their Christmas trees and colored lights around the windows. This year, we didn't need a Christmas tree or colored lights. We were aglow with the joy and pleasure we felt in the serenity of our new surroundings and the satisfaction of at last owning a home of our own.

We came back home and settled into bed quietly for the evening. Then at 12:29 a.m., Saturday, December 23, a tremendous rumbling began. The bed was shaking, the decorative tiles on the roof were rattling, and the refrigerator was thrown from one end of the kitchen to the other. An earthquake! This earthquake was measured at a magnitude of 6.2 and was destroying Managua. We quickly grabbed the sleeping girls and ran out into the street. Bricks and cement were tumbling around us. We could hear people screaming. We could see other people also running out of their houses. The twenty-five seconds of trembling felt like an eternity.

Francisco ran back and got the car, and we all piled into it. All morning long, aftershocks kept coming with small tremors every twenty minutes. We made one more trip into the house to get bottles and diapers for our two daughters. We tried to listen to the news on the radio in the car, but there was nothing but static. While the aftershocks kept coming, I tried to hide my fear from my children. I was singing and keeping them amused. We stayed in the car until 7:00 a.m., not knowing but fearing the worst. At last, Francisco and his father ventured out of the car and walked out to survey the neighborhood damage. When my father-in-law returned, his eyes were filled with tears and said, *"Everything is finished in Managua."* My husband had a somber look on his face and was completely silent. I knew that for my husband to be left speechless, he saw the utter devastation.

I slowly wandered back into the house. Everything was thrown on the floor, broken and scrambled. I tried to clean to make myself feel as if nothing had happened, but it was hopeless. As the hours went by, we saw more and more of the horror. People who had survived the initial earthquake but had gone back into their homes to retrieve something were killed by the aftershocks. The sixteen-year-old girl next door fell two stories to her death when she ran in the dark to escape down the stairs, but they had collapsed. Dead bodies were lying everywhere. There was a truckload of bodies piled one atop the other being hauled from a nearby prison. People were going crazy in the streets: looting, running with piles of fabric, armloads of lamps, mattresses, some laughing, and some crying.

The mortuaries ran out of coffins. People were using their upright closets to bury their relatives. And when the closets became scarce, even those were stolen by frantic people who would switch bodies in the boxes. Places were on fire, but there was no water to quench the flames. When the radio communication was reestablished, the instruction was to evacuate the city of Managua. The mass exodus began, but there was little or no gasoline available for cars. Rationing was immediately established, and people would stay in line for half a day to get gasoline.

The damage and devastation that the earthquake caused in Managua was innumerable. It killed ten thousand people and injured fifteen thousand. Of the seventy-four thousand homes that Managua had, fifty-three thousand (73 percent) were destroyed. All the orders of life in Nicaragua were disrupted. Hospitals and health centers were destroyed. Medical services were disorganized. Water systems were destroyed. Commercial activity was completely paralyzed for thirty days. Hotels, restaurants, movies, transportation, communication, small industries, etc. took more than two months to even begin to recover.

Our house was not structurally damaged, just very minor damage; however, we had to evacuate because the area was not safe. Houses around us had been destroyed as well as dead bodies. The area was contaminated. Fires broke out for which there was no water to put them out. We fled to the home of our good friends who were missionaries from the United States, Freddie and Aileen Crowe, and their two boys, Jonny and Paul. They lived about five miles outside Managua. As soon as I was able, I reported to work at Esso, and while I was working, my husband and Freddie helped assist needy people.

The earthquake brought astonishment, desperation, looting, and a mass exodus. In the blink of an eye, thousands of people from Managua died, or were forced into precarious conditions for survival. There was a nationwide concern directly after the quake of how to feed, shelter, and give medical care to the survivors. There was a generous fraternal attitude assumed by the people of several countries that responded immediately with a historical gesture of social kindness. El Salvador, Honduras, Canada, the United States and other countries sent canned food and medical supplies. In addition, personal individuals helped with the recovery. One in particular was the baseball hall of famer Roberto Clemente from Puerto Rico. Just before his death in 1972, Clemente put on a show in the 1971 World Series to help Pittsburgh defeat the favored Baltimore Orioles. Late in the 1972 season, he became the first Hispanic player to collect three thousand career hits (reference: www.Biography.com). Roberto Clemente sadly died in a plane crash flying to Nicaragua delivering goods to the survivors of the 1972 Nicaraguan earthquake.

Francisco and Freddie worked ceaselessly, providing food and water to earthquake survivors. Hundreds of survivors were homeless. With all the rationing, I learned to take a bath in one minute with only one gallon of water. I learned to appreciate water. We were using precious water to turn powdered milk into liquid milk for our two young girls. At times when I'm wasting water, I stop and I realize how very precious it is. We shouldn't wait for a disaster or draught to appreciate this wonderful liquid.

Besides the irreparable human losses that saddened the hearts of thousands of families, the Nicaraguan economy became seriously damaged. Managua, as the capital of Nicaragua, was the hub for main industrial and commercial source of the entire country and now the city was destroyed.

At first, I was nervous of going back to work because I didn't want to leave my family. But the love I had for them and my great desire to survive helped me overcome this fear. I gathered up courage to move out of the house, to accept the material losses, and tried to get back to some appearance of normalcy.

On December 24, Christmas Eve, I reported to work. I reported to the head of the company, Don Danilo Lacayo Rappaccioli also known as Engineer Danilo Lacayo as well as Dr. Danilo Lacayo (PhD). He is a member of INCAE Business School in Nicaragua. INCAE is also known as the Harvard sister school. He has performed a distinguished labor with ethic and success. He is a firm believer in continuous innovation. Don Danilo headed the construction of the refinery. This plant was the first petroleum refinery in Central America built in 1961.

When I reported to work, we were still experiencing aftershocks, and most people were still scattered in the outlying areas of the city. Many of those who were still nearby were frightened to report to work. I was the only business support available and found myself working for everyone. At work, we spent at least two weeks trying to find out how many employees had survived the earthquake.

Gasoline refined by Esso was of utmost importance in those days, and thus, I began working seven days a week and twelve hours a day. I was the only assistant/secretary, out of ten, who reported to work within twenty-four hours of the earthquake. I was the only one in my household in a position to earn a salary at this point because my husband, as an attorney, would have to wait until things returned to normal before he could resume his work. It was after forty days since the earthquake that we returned to our house. Things were beginning to become more orderly in the city. All the high-priced real estate in the area most affected by the earthquake completely lost its value, including our new house.

While going through this experience, I had many uncertainties. I had a panic of the earthquake itself because in its very essence is terrifying. I had apprehension of change because the earthquake forced me to leave my new house to live with some friends for an unknown length of time. I was anxious of losing what we had acquired only fifteen days before the earthquake, something which represented an accumulation of four years of our married life.

During this tragedy, my concern, above all things, was to protect the physical and mental health of our two daughters. Now after so many years, I asked my oldest daughter, Ilean Reineri, about her feelings as a three-year-old child going through the experience of a major earthquake. She said she did not feel any physical or mental disturbance. She only cared about having her parents near. She also felt confident because she always had shelter, food, and clothing. She recalls only part of the experience, moving from one house to another. In fact, the change was exciting to her because she was going to be with two little friends to play with, Jonny and Paul. She realized that so many people went through pain and sorrow, and she is so grateful her parents were careful about protecting her.

The earthquake of December 23, 1972, in Managua, Nicaragua, was a significant event in my life. Often, this sad time comes to mind but with gratitude. I'm so grateful I survived this major earthquake with my husband and my two girls. Now that the pain is gone, some things are remembered with amazement and incredulity. This earthquake meant, not only the physical shaking of the earth, but also a shaking of my reality: emotional anguish, leaving my home, long hours of work, as well as going through many learning experiences such as watching the stoicism of those who lost dear ones and material possessions.

Nations who respect the Mother
Nature deserve all kinds of respect!
—Mehmet Murat Ildan

CHAPTER 5

Illness

Health is not valued till sickness comes.
                                    —Thomas Fuller

Why is it that anytime you encounter a problem or an illness, you suddenly love waking up, suddenly you love and appreciate a sunset, or simply breathing? Seven months after the earthquake of 1972, I began to rapidly lose weight going down to ninety pounds. I'm only 5'2". I consulted a doctor to find the reason for my weight loss, but I was told, after multiple tests, that I was having a nervous breakdown due to the earthquake. After all the suffering and tragedy, many in

Nicaragua had been suffering from nervous breakdown. I knew that wasn't my case. I was sure something was wrong inside my body, not my mental health. I was sure it wasn't due to a nervous breakdown.

Not being satisfied with the diagnosis in Nicaragua, we went to Costa Rica for a second opinion. The doctors in Costa Rica performed a multitude of tests and discovered that I had a parasite, which in many cases is hard to detect until is too late. This parasite was likely a result of contaminated water. I started a treatment, but the recovery progression was long and arduous. I was skinny and tinny. I had low energy and no appetite. I was dehydrated and very weak. I would go to sleep, not knowing whether I was going to wake up in the morning. In fact, I was ready to die. I was unafraid. I knew my children would be fine. Francisco was the perfect father. I was so weak that the treatment was giving me side effects. The doctor decided to continue the same medication but at a very slow pace. He continued the treatment via intravenous that would take three to four hours on a daily schedule.

While I was experiencing this illness, I asked God, "*Why me, God? Why are things not working for me?*" I was, in fact, trying to tell God how to be God. Later, I realized that no matter what, we have to embrace God's way. That belief that if we follow Christ, nothing bad will happen to us is wrong! This illness encouraged me to grow spiritually every day.

Francisco was taking care of everything at this time as for me, it was a daily struggle to get out of bed. I was reluctant to eat because I was worried, I would get a parasite again. My doctor became concerned that I was not gaining weight because of my fear of eating contaminated food. Oddly enough, his advice was that if we were planning on having any more children, this would be a good time. As soon as I got pregnant, my appetite came back. In March 1975, our third child was born: Deborah Linda Baltodano. We were happy with our three girls.

If opening your eyes, or getting out of bed, or holding
a spoon, or combing your hair is the daunting
Mount Everest you climb today, that is okay.
—Carmen Ambrosio

CHAPTER 6

Careful What You Wish For

*Don't wish for elephants unless you own a zoo,
because wishes have a way of coming true.*
—Muppet Babies

This is a world of words. What I am writing is not new. A portion of my book was born out of an essay; in fact, a requirement while attending the University of San Francisco (USF) in California. My story is similar to the story of many other immigrants who have struggled but kept on moving with hope and determination. It is the story of adopting a new country. Adopting a country where my husband, our five daughters, and I would be safe and free.

It is a great challenge to share my life in a language that is not my native tongue as well as organizing my ideas and experiences. This story is about a tale of two countries and a family who has migrated to another country. The more I write the more I wonder. Why am I doing this? How can I make my story coherent? I know what to say, but my main goal is that those who read my story will be able to learn about my struggles and realize how God plans a person's life, or a whole family's life for a reason. Obviously, we all have a story to share. All the events, occurrences, and experiences, forced me, my husband, and my daughters to grow. When I look back into the years, I can honestly say it's been a wonderful journey, and I love all I've gone through.

When I say *be careful what you wish for; it may come true,* I really mean it. I was a teenager when I met Francisco, and we dated for six years before we got married. Even though we had initially decided we would marry after he graduated from law school, we got married before he graduated. We got married while he was attending his last year of law.

Now going back to the English language. Since childhood, I've been fascinated with the English language. I had a great desire to be fluent in English. Reading, writing, spelling, and punctuation was not a problem, but I was tongue-tied if I wanted to speak. I am so blessed because my Mom had a vision. At age six, I had an English teacher in Nicaragua that would come to my house once a week: Ms. Lydia Gilmore. She was a tall, heavy, curly, black long hair perhaps late fifties or early sixties. I remember her wearing most of the time a black dress, which is warm for a tropical, hot, and humid weather in Nicaragua. I also remember she had a peculiar body scent. Even though I had the essential and basic English knowledge, my dream was to have a command of the language and be able to speak fluently, but it was hard because I didn't have the opportunity to communicate regularly in English.

I remember being a child and pretending I was fluent in English. I would sing English songs fantasizing I was conducting a conversation. I would recite, not sing, Paul Anka's song, "Put Your Head on My Shoulder" and "Dreamin" with Johnny Burnette. In many instances, I didn't understand the lyrics of the song, but I just liked it. I just did it phonetically. Now, I am fluent in the English language although with an accent. I don't want to change it because I sound different from the rest. Now, this is why I say *be careful what you wish for.*

I always had in my mind the desire to go to USA for a short time to take an intense course in English but with no intention to leave Nicaragua. It hasn't been easy running the race with five daughters in a new country, new culture, and new language. Life got more complex when I got redirected. There is a big difference between being a tourist and being a citizen. I just wanted to learn English. I was happy and loved my country.

Oh well, be careful what you wish for. The Sandinista revolution brought me to the United States of America. But I didn't come to the USA by accident. What was meant for harm, he turned it into an advantage. I ended up in California. I have been so blessed. Just keep in mind you might be taken to a place you never expected, but no doubt, life is so unpredictable. Have faith that you are precisely where you are supposed to be.

Be careful what you wish for, you'll probably get it.
—Proverb

A Map Showing the Route from Nicaragua to Northern California

The route from Nicaragua to Northern California
took us over all of Central America through Mexico
and up to Northern California our final destiny.

Visas while crossing countries on our journey.

CHAPTER 7

Crossing the Border

*There comes a time when one must take a position
that is neither safe, nor politic, nor popular; but, he
must take it because conscience tells him it is right.*
                                        —Martin Luther King Jr.

In May 1979, I had started my fourth year of law but only attended classes for two weeks because the political situation had worsened. So, we decided to move our vacation date to California to June instead of August and left our country hoping we would soon be back. We departed on Saturday, June 2, 1979. We left our domestic employees, Sara, Pablo, and their two daughters, in charge of the house. We paid their wages in advance, provided them with cash for miscellaneous expenses as well as left the payment for the electricity and the water bills.

The plan was that instead of flying, we would drive, and we would first stop at El Salvador. Francisco contacted his missionary friend he had known in Nicaragua. The calling of my husband and my father-in-law, who was also a lawyer, was to help and guide North American missionaries who came to the country regardless of their religious denomination.

When the earth shook in 1972, we fled with two daughters. Then the earth shook again with the Sandinista revolution, and we fled with four daughters. We left our beautiful house and everything we had worked for since our marriage. Obviously, we had options: to stay and fight, or flee. We fled to a destination four thousand miles away to protect our daughters.

We spent three days in El Salvador making minor repairs to our vehicle and taking care of Kattya's high fever due to a cold. Kattya was nine months old. God took care of us while crossing the borders of Honduras, El Salvador, Guatemala, Mexico, and the U.S.

We traveled on our pickup truck instead of our car. It was convenient though still scary knowing we were going to drive through hostile places. When we settled in our compact red truck with a fastened camping trailer, we were happy and unquestionably in denial hoping that things would be back to normal in a few weeks. We were going on vacation to El Salvador to visit our American missionary friends. The red truck was full: my husband, Francisco; our four daughters, Ilean Reineri (nine), Claudia Graciela (seven), Deborah Linda (four), Kattya Francis (nine months old); and I, who was six months pregnant. Way within my heart, I had fear and apprehension.

I continually questioned myself. What will happen to my house? What will happen to my country? And most of all, what will happen to us? Nicaragua was going to go on a major strike in a few days on Monday, June 4, 1979.

While crossing Honduras, El Salvador, Guatemala, and Mexico, we were treated well (thank God) possibly because of our four young daughters. The customs personnel in all the countries we crossed asked, *"Are you running away from the Sandinista revolution?"*

We arrived to my sister's house in Daly City, California, on July 11, 1979. A short time later, after we arrived in California on July 17, Somoza left the country and fled to Miami, and later, he exiled to Paraguay. On July 19, the Sandinista National Liberation Front (FSLN) entered Managua and hundreds of thousands of Nicaraguan celebrated their triumph. This civil war left approximately fifty thousand dead and approximately 150,000 Nicaraguan in exile.

We were advised not to go back to Nicaragua. My husband knew some of the Sandinista's leaders. Some had attended law school with him, and he also knew their ideologies. One powerful reason for not going back was that my husband had been appointed district attorney for the city of Managua, and the Sandinistas were taking retaliation against people who had any position connected with the overturned Somoza government. Even though my husband wasn't in politics, his position was considered a political position. When we decided not to go back to Nicaragua, it was certainly a very risky decision, but we had to move forward. Leaving Nicaragua was painful and difficult, but we decided not to go back. The Sandinista revolution drove us into Northern California without knowing this was going to be our refuge, our safe place, and our future.

When we arrived to California, most people thought that the Sandinista's triumph was a good change. It was so painful that I left behind my parents, friends, home, and country. While Francisco and I were very close, at times together, we would not say a single word. We were so quiet. I felt as if we didn't want to think about anything. It was a weird sentiment. Obviously, we had to start all over again. At this time, so many professionals from the middle class and above had left Nicaragua. The country was losing so many medical doctors, lawyers, and engineers. At this moment in our lives, we had to plan for the right course of action in another country. At that time, I had to suspend my fourth year of law school. I would have been class of 1980. Francisco had to suspend his career as a lawyer in Nicaragua. We didn't know where to begin with four daughters: nine, seven, four, and nine months old and myself, six months pregnant. We had been visiting California every year for a three-week vacation, but this time, it looked as if this vacation was going to last longer. We had stayed with my sister for forty days, and later, we moved to an apartment.

While staying at my sister's, some days I would weep quietly while hugging my husband. I was so pregnant with my fifth child. I was sobbing and asking him what are we going to do? Francisco would say, "*Don't worry. Remember, if God is for us, who can be against us?*" (Romans 8:31). I don't know who said this, but I like it. "*Having children changes the way you live but also changes* why *you live.*"

Those days, while on vacation, were not enjoyable days for me. Francisco always looked relaxed and confident. I don't know; perhaps, he possibly was just pretending to make me feel good and give me support. His burden was gigantic as well as his faith. The responsibility to take care of four little children and a pregnant wife were immeasurable. I felt so safe with him. All I wanted was to be with my husband and my children. Families are meant to be together. Separating families is inhuman and criminal.

Our vacation was a temporary exciting situation but residing in another country was a difficult challenging experience. But in reality, did it matter where I ended up.

On September 18, 1979, at the University of California in the San Francisco Medical Center/Moffitt Hospital, I had another baby! Guess. Baby girl: Lilette Jill Baltodano.

Upon our arrival to California, we were forced to live off our savings. My husband opened a bank in California one year before our marriage. He was a firm believer in saving. I used to say to him, "*You are a penny saver.*" But in reality, Francisco was saving during the years of bounty and planned for the years of famine. Although we had not foreseen what the future had in store for us, he was guided in this action. "*All things work well for those who love the Lord*" (Romans 8:28).

When you read this memoir, you will see that change is good even though you will go through some grieving but don't grieve too long. You need to move on. God can do the impossible.

Keep on reading, there is more to come while *still on vacation.*

It was while we were starting our long journey and still in Nicaraguan soil that we noticed our two oldest girls were getting sick. We were able to figure out that through the truck's tailpipe, the exhaust and fumes were reaching inside the bed of the truck where Ilean and Claudia were sitting. The girls were getting poisoned from the fumes hence feeling nauseous and sick. We stopped in a town called Jinotega, which is about eighty-eight miles from Managua so that Francisco could get the car repaired and continue our journey.

Although not free from complications, I felt that God took care of us while crossing Central America, Mexico, and finally driving across the border into the United States. While driving across the borders, we decided to stay neutral and did not discuss politics to avoid confrontation. When you are traveling with children, you have to be extremely careful.

After nine long days of driving in a small truck with four children and one on the way, it was on June 9, 1979, that we crossed Mexico through the Mexicali border into the United State of America. Our vacation was planned to hopefully be for only three weeks. As we went through the American customs and the immigration officer stamped a six-month visa in my passport, I immediately made it clear to her that we didn't need a six-month visa. I explained to her that we were just visiting for a short time. I firmly believed that the situation in Nicaragua would eventually be all right. The officer explained that a six-month visa was part of an automatic process for tourists.

A year before this vacation, during the Christmas of 1978, we spent a few days in Costa Rica with our missionary friends, Freddie and Aileen. During our visit with them, rumors of a revolution had been swirling, and they very kindly offered, "*If the revolution comes, send your two oldest daughters, Ilean and Claudia, to Tennessee.*" Freddie and Aileen were scheduled to go on furlough back to Chattanooga, Tennessee, around June/July of the following year—1979.

Of course, at that time, the idea of a revolution was an unlikely occurrence to us. The Somoza government looked strong in power, but alas, the revolution did arrive, and we sent our two oldest daughters to Chattanooga. Though our two daughters were still young, only nine and seven years old, they were strong, and somehow, they realized what we were going through. The two youngest, Deborah (four years old) and Kattya (nine months old), stayed with us while expecting the arrival of our fifth baby.

It was so emotional when we left Ilean and Claudia at the San Francisco International Airport. Letting go of two of our daughters was hard but also provided a sense of peace of mind because they were going to stay with a good family, and we would be able to concentrate on the arrival of the new baby and organize our uncertain stay in the country. It was later that we realized that while Ilean and Claudia were supposedly mature for their age, the separation affected them. They stayed in Tennessee with our friends for six long months. It was a challenging experience, and it forced both of them to grow. They left in August and returned to California in December along with a newly acquired cute Southern accent.

When they returned, I promised myself I would never send them away. We arrived to California together and then the family got separated for way too long—six months. How can I criticize those mothers who leave their children behind? The expectation is that a mother is to raise and nurture them, not to send them away, or leave them behind. I'm sorry, Ilean and Claudia.

The bottom line is that immigrants, legal or undocumented, come to this land of *milk and honey* with hope, for safety, and for a better life. Why should we be alarmed of refugees? Let's not be paranoid. Let's not be anxious of our neighbors. For heaven's sake, our neighbors are at risk. There is no invasion of people. They are looking for safety. Our neighbors live in poor nations.

In addition, there are 1.2 million young people in this country who all they know is the USA. They are hurting. For these kids, America is their country. They have no recollection of their country of birth. These kids are grieving. When I hear, "Get out of my country," in a despicable manner, it is so painful and offensive. We live in the most powerful nation in the world. I am so disturbed because this is very personal to me. People are hurting.

The United States of America has a beautiful history, but some people want to change it with bigotry and hate. Silence is complicity. We have to raise our voices. It is so painful when I hear that in this country, we are separating children from families who are coming to seek asylum. These are families seeking protection. Children should not be separated from their parents. Families are to stay together. The trauma children suffer with separation is indescribable. Separating children from their families creates long-term damage to the children. In addition, they are separated without appropriate process to reunite them with their parents. It is a shame on those who separate children from their families. This cruel activity is a disgrace and a dishonor to this country whose bountiful shores have always received those seeking asylum and protection.

Obviously, we left everything we had worked for behind in Nicaragua, which meant that we had to start all over again. Leaving your country is a painful and difficult decision. If we had gone back to Nicaragua, Francisco's arrest would have been imminent because the Sandinista government could easily fabricate criminal charges, so we decided to stay.

In October 1979, my husband started working for Prudential Insurance. While he was working, I stayed home with Deborah (four years old), Kattya (one year old), and our brand-new baby, Lilette. Throughout the day and with the little time I had free, I kept reflecting: *We have five children. We need to organize our life in the United States. We need to bring back from Tennessee Ilean Reineri and Claudia Graciela. We need to move out of this apartment. It's too small for a family of seven, and the landlord won't allow us to stay as a family of seven. We have to find a house. We don't need a fancy one, but it has to be bigger.* In my mind, there was always the burden, the anxiety that I had to find a job, but I asked myself, *What kind of job? A full-time or a part-time job? Will I be able to handle it? I'm not fluent in English, but I am good at taking risks. Who will take care of the kids? Oh well, it will be okay. I know we will find someone.* I would start whispering to God, "*Lord, tell me, where am I going and how to get there? I feel defenseless.*"

We kept praying and started looking for a house. Finally, we found the ideal house. This was a three-bedroom house, living room, dining room, large family room, kitchen, three bathrooms, and a two-car garage. It was located in San Bruno, California, on top of a hill with a beautiful view. And the owners of this house also had five children, but now they had already retired and ready to live in a smaller house.

Because of our recent arrival to this country, we had not established credit, and in order to close the deal to buy this house, the loan company required a cosigner. That was a big problem. Even though we were new to the area, fortunately, we had friends, and among those friends was a Nicaraguan girl who had been my very close friend and married to a successful pioneer of one of the world's largest family-owned companies. I remember I called her and shared our situation with her. They helped us as cosigners, and of course, the deal to buy the house went through without a problem.

When you are in a journey, you have to be prepared and willing to go. I had to stop holding up to memories and learn to let some things to go. The things I left behind. I had to stick to my new life and let go of my past. I had to let go of the material things I left behind. But it didn't happen automatically. I am not trying to preach but sharing what worked for me. To grow and to mature takes time and a lot of work. It takes discipline. It takes a lot of praying, a lot of meditating, breathing in and out, laughing, and drinking a lot of water.

> *Take risks. If you win, you will be happy;*
> *if you lose, you will be wise.*
> —Anonymous

This was my identity as I lived my
life between two cultures.

CHAPTER 8

Between Two Cultures

No culture can live if it attempts to be exclusive.
—Mahatma Gandhi

It may appear to some that I am a less-advantaged person because by migrating to the United States of America, I have become part of a minority group, or a USA subculture; however, by my own standards, I feel that I have faced so many challenges and have added such experience to my life that I am more advantaged than many others, and now I am able to analyze and understand some of the barriers between cultures. But in fact, what some might perceive as a disadvantage, in actuality, it became my advantage.

I was born in Nicaragua. While in school, I did very well scholastically, and although I was not voted the-most-popular girl, I formed lasting friendships, which I could turn to in trying times. I graduated from high school; I started working for Esso refinery. In 1968, I became a wife, and in 1969, I was a mother. Later, I started law school, and I found myself handling several roles and doing well in my culture. My husband was a lawyer, and we both were able to maintain a home and a staff to help with household responsibilities. In my opinion, the pace in my life was orderly and established. When I migrated to the United States of America in 1979, I was forced into a new culture.

I have since found that human beings are very much alike in many ways: they all cry, become excited, laugh, and eat. But also, I have found how profoundly different they are in the sense that their behavior is modified by culture. A very simple example could be when one is hungry. In my case, I enjoy rice and beans, whereas a large number of native-born Californians might satisfy their hunger with a hamburger or a pizza.

The American diet is varied due to the influence of immigrants from all parts of the world. Food is abundant, rich in calories, tasty, and many times, easy to prepare. The diet in America is incredibly abundant, such as Irish stew, chop suey, goulash, chile con carne, ravioli, sauerkraut, Yorkshire pudding, welsh rarebit, Spanish omelets, English muffins, caviar, mayonnaise, antipasto, gruyère cheese, Danish pastry, Canadian bacon, hot tamales, scones, Turkish coffee, minestrone, filet mignon, and many, many more. It's so interesting the origin of certain foods: The Germans brought hamburgers and sausages. The Dutch taught us how to make waffles and doughnuts. The Italians brought pizza, spaghetti, and ravioli. The Irish brought their famous stew. The Chinese brought egg rolls, chow mein, etc.

In Nicaragua, grains such as rice, corn, and beans constitute about 75 percent of the people's diet. There is an ironic situation between the comparisons of diets in that most Americans are so well-fed that they consequently have serious health problems; on the other hand, in some countries, the biggest health problem is due to malnutrition.

Besides comparing how human beings differ in the foods they eat, there are also two factors that have helped in my integration into this culture: time and communication. I have learned that every culture has its own pace and tempo and that the style of every culture does not have a genetic origin; it can be learned.

I regard time as the principal rhythm of a culture. In Latin America, most people take precedence over schedules; there is no major worry about the clock. There is always *mañana*—tomorrow. Schedules, most of the time, are not met, and there is a proliferation of unfinished jobs. By way of illustration, if a relative or a friend comes to visit or comes to request help or advice, I have to hear them out. I cannot excuse myself just because I have a schedule to meet. That would be a terrible insult. On the other hand, in the North American culture, schedules and routines are of primary importance. People live closely attached to the time, and there is a high level of stress and anxiety. In the United States, some people get upset if you do not call them ahead of time and let them know you will be visiting them even if you are close friends. Invitation to parties has a time specified for arrival and even departure.

The other factor that played an important role in my adjustment is communication. It is the process by which human interaction takes place. I learned English in Nicaragua, but I did not have the opportunity to practice expressing myself, and now in the United States, I discovered that I have more ability than I thought. I have learned that an older person adjusts more slowly to a social group as I compare the development of my children and my own. In a short period, my children learned to speak English fluently while I am still struggling with a heavy accent. I feel like a computer that was programmed in Spanish and now has to change its software. However, that is easier said than done.

As a member of the American subculture, I have learned to participate in the way of life of the larger society as well as my own subgroup. Through my different roles, I have learned to look at things from a different perspective. I had to accept new ways of doing things. I have to have an open mind to think biculturally and bilingually in order to improve my everyday learning process. I compare the learning of another culture to learning about another person; it takes time to adjust to a culture, and I have to accept its way of doing things. I have been motivated to grow personally in this society because of my job, my studies, and dealings with other people. Through my job at Chevron, I had the opportunity to interact with a broad spectrum of people, learn on a day-by-day basis more about its culture, and improve my communication skills as well as to have the satisfaction of being a useful member of this society. Through my studies, I was able to pick up where I left off when I departed from my country. When I consider the many cultural experiences I have gone through, I realize that my personal growth is continuously improving. Learning is a lifelong activity!

What is the culture of the United States? Can we typify an American personality or its customs? Can we identify and analyze differences and similarities between a particular culture and the USA culture? The United States is a nation where different cultures and languages converge. People have come to the United States from all over the world. It has often been given many metaphoric names such as *The Promised Land, A Nation of Immigrants*, and *A Melting Pot* among many others. Most historians and some economists agree that the USA has benefited from the surge of immigrants who have come to its bountiful shores. It is for this reason that it is so hard to pinpoint the culture of the United States. If we trace back to 1607 when the first colony was settled in Jamestown, Virginia, its settlers were Europeans, mostly British subjects, who were fleeing political and religious persecutions in their own land. This thus become the humble beginning of a great nation that grew 212 million in less than four hundred years.

Spanish settlers also came to an area they later called Reyno de Castilla del Oro in 1552—now known as Latin America—at the time inhabited by native indigenous tribes with their colorful customs and culture, which changed after the arrival of the Spanish conquerors. Spain ruled for three hundred years, but after the success of the American and French Revolutions, colonists wanted their freedom.

When the people of Latin America became free, they did not unite like the people of the United States. Communications were poor. It was difficult for people to reach one another. Separate little nations were formed. In the beginning, many of the new countries tried to draw up constitutions or plans of government like that of the United States. However, most of the people were poor. They could not read or write and could not understand what their leaders were doing. After a while, the new nations came to be ruled by dictators. The people had few rights even though they were free from their European rulers.

My country, Nicaragua, is located in this area. It is the largest of the Central American republics, and we find that 70 percent of the population is mestizo (of mixed European and aboriginal ancestry), 17 percent of European ancestry, 9 percent black, and 4 percent native indigenous. And the culture is, as can be expected from its varied ancestry and conquerors, mixed. Nicaragua is an underdeveloped nation, but people refer to these countries as developing nations because it sounds positive and acceptable. Nicaragua has a history of prolonged political turmoil between its two parties: liberals and conservatives. A large segment of the population is impoverished because of its weak economy, political instability, plus nature has dealt it blows with severe earthquakes. To a large degree, its economy is dependent on agriculture. The hot weather, the rainy growing season, and the dry harvest time are good for growing sugar cane. In the hot and damp lowlands, there are plantations of bananas. Coffee is grown in the highlands. Many people live in farms, and they raise the crops that fill their needs: beans, corn, and potatoes.

I just mentioned that Nicaragua is the largest of the Central American republics, but geographically comparing Nicaragua with United States, Nicaragua has 50,193 square miles with an approximate population of 2,312,000, and the United States has 3,615,123 square miles with an approximate population of 219,250,000.

Nicaraguans enjoy summer weather all year round. The weather is hot and humid, and we have two seasons: six months of dry season and six months of rainy season. The rainy season brings floods, and the dry season bakes the land. Even though Nicaragua has tropical weather, there are some cities, located in the mountains, that enjoy cooler climate. The average temperature throughout the year is 80 degrees. At night, one sleeps under a light blanket. Thank God, Nicaragua has only two seasons because there is a lot of poverty, and people cannot afford adequate shelter and clothing; whereas in the United States, I am amazed at the beautiful four seasons of the year: how the flowers spring in one season, and how the leaves fall in another, how people go crazy during the summer eating outdoors, picnics in parks, backyard barbecues, and how surprised I was when I saw the snow. I knew snow was white from books and poets but never thought that whiteness could blind me. I also like these beautiful four seasons of the year because it allows you to wear different fashions for every season.

What have I learned? Among the many things, I have learned that we all have 1,440 minutes to spend each day; this includes the rich, the poor, the president, and the peasant, the people from Nicaragua, and the people from the United States. What I have learned from this culture is how to better spend or make use of those 1,440 minutes. If possible, do two things at one time. Read while having a haircut. Listen to music or interesting tape while washing dishes, driving, bathing, etc. Always have a paper and pen handy. Write whatever comes to one's mind. One should never trust memory. Use early-morning and late-evening hours, the most quiet and uninterrupted hours of the day. This is a good way of getting ahead in life. Plan the day at its beginning. Keep good traces. Use waiting time or travel time. Delegate work; do not do what someone else can do for you. Sleep on purpose. Decide how much sleep you need. Plan your worry time; this will keep you from worrying while you are busy. And last but not least, breathe in and breathe out.

While in Nicaragua, everything is more relaxed; in the United States, there are all these deadlines to be met, and jobs to be done. I had to keep up with this pace to which I was not accustomed. I had to adapt my Latin culture into the American practicality of getting several things done at a time. I'm sure that if I return to my home country, after so many years since 1979 in the United States, I would experience reintegration problems and would have to go through a period of adjustment—for instance, the weather, the diet, the pace of doing things, starting new friendships, etc.

What is my identity? Do I have to forget my ethnic background? In the U.S., I have been able to meet and been able to learn from so many different races, religions, cultures as well as so many different foods and different ways of thinking. I have learned that in order to understand a new culture, I must not judge conditions according to the precepts of my culture, but I must accept this culture as it is practiced, adopting those customs, which will enrich my life and my family's, and discarding those, which might not agree with my ethical standards.

Somewhere I heard that Latinos are not capable of assimilating into the American culture and that Latinos create danger and division. That is totally wrong. My family is an asset to this country. We have contributed to this country as well as innumerable immigrants and children of immigrants. We didn't come with wealth but with the spirit of dignity and respect. *Somewhere I heard* immigrants are drug dealers, rapists, and criminals. I don't hear, honest, industrious, or hardworking. Immigrants come to America in search of safety, security, and jobs.

Cultures might be different, but they are loud, filled with disappointments, responsibilities, and problems. Life is full of change, which is the only real constant we will experience. Life is a constant combination of good and bad events where we have to make informed decisions. Initially, this vacation has been a challenging adventure, but what has happened in the long run has been an incredible amount of experience that I will always value as a gold mine. Let's pray that there will continue to be room for all of us while we are transported throughout life in different vehicles.

Although my move from Nicaragua to the United States has been an adventure and one that may be an exciting opportunity for some, I initially had to adapt. Even though I was able to understand English language, knowledge is not a substitute for cultural understanding; both are needed. Initially, I felt insecure in this new environment: adapting to the new language and being separated from close relatives and friends lengthened the process of adjustment.

*Preservation of one's own culture does not require
contempt or disrespect for other cultures.*
—Cesar Chavez

For it is by grace you have been saved, through faith—
and this is not from yourselves, it is the gift of God.
—Ephesians 2:8

CHAPTER 9

My Position on Faith

Faith is taking the first step even when
you don't see the whole staircase.
—Martin Luther King Jr.

As I am writing, I am reflecting on God's work in my life and in the life of my family. I must open my heart and praise him.

Since the beginning of time, people have always been searching for meaning and yearning for assurance that life has a purpose and that death is not the end. There have been many gods that have been adopted according to patterns of culture: Worship of the sun and nature. Egyptians worshipped the Nile River and the sun. Osiris was one of the most important gods of ancient Egypt. Worship of animals. Many looked upon animals as possessing remarkable power and conveying wisdom, fertility, and strength. Kings, thought of as divinities, built pyramids of rare beauty and great size to entomb themselves with their earthly treasures. Also, there have been many faiths, a lot of them now lost, but each, in its era, was a striking example of mankind's ceaseless search for meaning. As I read about these faiths and look back and analyze my personal life, I see my own searching to find a fulfilling and enriching spiritual experience.

I was born and raised in the Roman Catholic religion. I was a devout follower of that faith, unquestioningly believing its dogma and practicing its many rites. In Nicaragua, over 90 percent of the population is a member of a Christian denomination. Approximately 73 percent of Nicaraguans follow the Roman Catholic religion. I was part of the majority of Nicaraguans raised Catholic even though my Dad was agnostic.

As a teenager, I was interested in the Baptist/evangelical doctrine. It is incredible how this upset my Dad even though he was a humanist nonbeliever. My Mom, a devote Catholic, respected my decision without any comments. The Catholic Church has progressed, but when I was a teenager, Catholics had no direct access to the Bible, and the mass was celebrated in Latin. I remember as a teenager I asked the priest of the church I attended, Iglesia del Carmen, why we believed in so many things that didn't make any sense and weren't in the Bible. I pointed out a few things mentioned in the Bible that didn't agree with the Catholic doctrine. He didn't answer my questions. He just took the Bible away from me. I was so disappointed and saddened, and I kept this incident to myself for many years. Now, I am glad the Catholic Church has evolved in many areas.

Conformity to culture, especially during the period of childhood, is indeed a factor that determines the religion of an individual. I realize now that during my childhood, I was identifying myself with my schoolmates, my family, and society by being a Catholic, and this gave me security, affection, and approval. When I learned to participate in the Catholic rites, I did so without questioning before I learned the corresponding explanation of their purpose. I accepted my religion along with the rituals because I felt safe, and it was familiar to me. While putting these thoughts on paper, I discovered many interesting things about myself. One of my findings is that during my childhood and adolescence, I attended an all-girl school, which I assume created and developed in my personality a great bashfulness toward males.

Even though I was raised in the Roman Catholic religion, my parents had conflicting beliefs. My father was forever worrying about achieving the freedom of the proletariat, seeking a true social change, and the establishment of a classless society. He spent most of his time reading Marx and other socialist books and writing protest poems, which caused him imprisonment for a whole year in Nicaragua. My mother, a dedicated Catholic, was always praying to the Virgin Mary and her favorite saints and, of course, lighting candles to them as a demonstration of her faithfulness.

I recall the great influence the Catholic Church had upon me. I still remember the majesty of the church structures, sitting in a pew, and kneeling down to worship God, the Virgin Mary, and the Saints. On the walls around the church, the fourteen Stations of the Cross through which Jesus had to pass sorrowfully on his way to Golgotha, are still vivid in my mind. I also remember reciting the Rosary: one *Lord's Prayer* between each set of ten *Hail Mary's* that my mother gave me when I received my First Communion.

After five years of educating myself through readings of the Bible and visiting a Baptist Church, I decided to become a member. I am aware that it is neither a religion nor a church that will give me an inner personal experience, but in my search to find a fulfilling and enriching spiritual experience, I felt the necessity of fellowship. As a result of my involvement with the evangelical, my beliefs conflicted, not only with my family, but also with my friends who were all Roman Catholic. To most of my friends, I was an apostate, a traitor, and a deserter because of my religious beliefs.

The opportunity to become acquainted with the doctrine taught by the Baptist Church, which is based on the Bible, not tradition, or rites, gave me a stronger state of spiritual identity but also contentment to the point that the adversities I faced in life have served to strengthen my faith. I clearly remember when I was pregnant almost on my ninth month expecting my first baby. I went shopping looking for baby clothes and baby articles. I was at the baby store, *La Miniatura*, and this lady, who was also visiting the store, had known me since I was a child but suddenly started talking to me very loudly in front of the other customers saying that I was an apostate and a traitor for leaving the Catholic religion. As she talked, I felt the blood rise to my face and my heart pound, and of course, all eyes were on me. I tried to remain calm and tried a couple of quiet breaths. Out of respect, I just pretended she wasn't talking to me. As I walked away, I felt hurt and humiliated.

I found the Baptist faith less concerned with ritualism and filled with sound teachings based on the Bible. I learned that the Bible is the only infallible rule of faith and conduct that everyone is allowed and encouraged to read the Bible and that the Holy Spirit alone can aid in the true interpretation of the Word of God. This devotion is crucial to the point that man is justified by faith and not by works. By reading the Bible, I became aware that it is not a religion, not a church, not a lodge, not good works, nothing, or no one, but Jesus saves. "*For whosoever shall call upon the name of the Lord shall be saved*" (Romans 10:13).

I have found that adversity is not a crisis one can avoid, but a situation, which one must deal with. Adversity at times can seem impossible to overcome. It never comes at a convenient time, and when it does occur, it may be overwhelming. However, learning to face seemingly insurmountable problems has given me an opportunity to discover my weaknesses and has helped me grow stronger spiritually, mentally, and physically.

In 1972 while in Nicaragua, two of my daughters were hospitalized. They were very close to death due to gastroenteritis, which is a serious intestinal infection. The doctors later told me that if their situation had not improved by a certain time, they would have died of dehydration. This experience taught me that no one can truly understand death until faced with it. Even though, death must come to each and every one of us. Death is an experience we all will have to deal with sooner or later. No one is singled out for this event; it is devastating, tragic, and strikes all.

The adversities I have gone through in my life have given me an opportunity to see my frail human weaknesses as well as the necessity of a spiritually secure life, particularly while going through hard times, more so than when everything is running smoothly.

In my own searching to find a fulfilling and enriching inner personal life, my conclusion is that a person is made of body, mind, and soul; and as each of us feeds her or his body and mind, the soul must also be nourished. I also believe that the individual who drives out God drives out her or his own soul, and without a soul, an individual cannot survive. That life has a purpose and that death is not the end of existence. That if life has a purpose, we should live in such a way that yesterday's problems will be more easily solved today, and that my spiritual growth should be for the benefit of and in service to others.

There is a wise and beautiful passage in the Bible that says, "*Train up a child in the way he should go, and when he is old, he will not depart from it*" (Proverbs 22:6). Yet I am aware that at a certain moment in my daughter's individual lives, they must choose their own spiritual identity as I did.

I enjoy and never get tired of reading the Bible. I am always amazed at its contents and beautiful language. Even though it took over 1,600 years and forty God-inspired men to compose it. (2 Timothy 3:16-17)

Do for others just what you want them to do for you.
—Luke 6:31

CHAPTER 10

Political Assessment

Loyalty to a country, always.
Loyalty to a government, only *when it deserves it.*
—Mark Twain

Threatening political clouds began gathering in Nicaragua in the early 1960s. By 1979, they had grown darker and more dangerous and resulted in the overthrow of the Somoza dynasty. The revolution was fed by international sources including Cuba, Russia, Venezuela, and Mexico. This volatile political situation forced me to first take a political stand by withdrawing from any active political involvement and finally resulted in leaving my country for the safety of my family, which I initially thought it was going to be for a short time hoping that after just a three-week vacation out of my country, everything will be back to normal.

The three major ideologies of the world: communism, socialism, and capitalism, whether philosophical, political, or economic, have some relation in my present political beliefs. Communism is based upon the writings of Karl Marx and Friedrich Engels, nineteenth century philosophers, but was truly developed, polished, and implemented by Vladimir Ilich Ulyanov, otherwise known as Lenin. *"Communist thinkers are convinced that the Marxian inspiration and its Leninist modification are always perfectly harmonious. Noncommunist thinkers feel that some Leninist positions contradict Marx in spirit if not in letter"* (Ebenstein, William. *Today's ISMS*. Englewood Cliffs, NJ: Prentice-Hall Inc., 1970, pp. 30–31)

According to Marx, the history of mankind has been a story of class struggle. Marx wrote in *The Communist Manifesto*:

Freeman and slave, patrician and plebeian, lord and serf…in a word, oppressor and oppressed, stood in constant opposition to one another…a fight that each time ended, either in a revolutionary reconstitution of society at large, or in the common ruin of the contending classes.

Harold J. Laski on *The Communist Manifesto* (New York: Random House Inc., 1967, pp. 131–132). The two hostile classes that Marx mentions are the bourgeois (the property owner) and the proletarians (the working class). As author Harry B. Ellis says in his book *Ideal and Ideologies* (Cleveland: The World Publishing Co., 1968, p. 50), communism shows two faces to the world, and he quotes Milovan Djilas saying, "Begins always as a movement of highest idealism and selfless sacrifice, attracting into its ranks the most gifted, the bravest, and even the most noble intellects of the nation… Why? Because…, continued the Yugoslav leader…communism promises care and protection for the young and tender respect for the old…selfless love, comradeship, solidarity."

The face which communism presents to the noncommunist world is completely different for the people under communist domination elsewhere. This is the terrible truth of communism and also of military dictatorships in Latin America. Yet the facade communism presents to the countries that embrace this ideology is one of sweetness and light. Djilas says, *"Communist ideals exist only while the movement is young, before it has tasted the fruits of power."* Of himself and many others, Arthur Koestler says, *"We ex-Communists are the only ones on your side who know what it's all about"* (Ellis, Harry B. *Ideal and Ideologies.* Cleveland: The World Publishing Co., 1968, p. 50).

The writings of Karl Marx and Friedrich Engels produced the system called socialism. Many affirm that in the Bible, we can find the first signs of socialism and that the early Christians preached socialism in their everyday lives. The communists speak of socialism as *"a stage on the road to communism"* (Ellis, Harry B. *Ideal and Ideologies.* Cleveland: The World Publishing Co., 1968, p. 29).

Although socialism does not defend extinction of private property, it is evident that it is against social inequality (Ellis, Harry B. in *Ideals and Ideologies.* Cleveland: The World Publishing Co., 1968, p. 130). *"All this has given rise to the stereotype that a Socialist is 'pink' and a Communist is 'red.' Place Socialists in power and they will tend to turn redder."* But history indicates otherwise. Democratic socialists were in power for most of the last thirty years in West Germany, and this did not happen. Socialists *"seek power by ballots rather than bullets, and once in office they know they are not for keeps, but are subject to being voted out in the next election... Once in power, Communists are determined to stay there indefinitely"* (Ebenstein, William. *Today's ISMS.* Englewood Cliffs: Prentice-Hall Inc., 1970, p. 249).

But even though communists and democratic socialists go separate ways, both sides continue to look toward Marx's writing for inspiration. While communists and socialists are members of one definitive political party, capitalists may be democrat or republican or belong to no party at all. Capitalism, in other words, is an economic term, not a political party affiliation. For most communist-oriented people, capitalism stands for exploitation. Capitalism is *"an economic system in which the means of production and distribution are mostly privately owned and operated for private profit"* (*Funk & Wagnalls*

Standard Desk Dictionary [Lippincott & Crowell, Publishers, 1983, Volume 1, p. 92]).

Communists argue such a system exploits working people. The capitalist disagrees with this hypothesis because in the business world's view, the competition for the consumer's dollar protects the public. According to this system, supply and demand set a value on all goods and services offered. The capitalist doctrine was known as *laissez-faire*, literally *"Let (people) do (what they choose)"* (Ellis, Harry B. *Ideal and Ideologies.* Cleveland: The World Publishing Co., 1968, p. 174). The capitalist differs from the socialist, who favors government planning and some nationalization, and from the communist, who advocates one-party control and almost total public ownership. With the capitalist doctrine, business people, like other human beings, try to gain as much advantage for them as they can.

The laissez-faire extreme doctrine of capitalism has now practically disappeared from the modern world. For example, car manufacturers must include safety features in their automobiles, factories must control smoke pouring out from their chimneys, laws exist to protect natural resources, and the government has a law that controls minimum wages to ensure unskilled workers are guaranteed a reasonable share of the economic wealth. *"We have seen how far the United States has moved from laissez-faire capitalism, in the realm of regulatory laws to protect the health and well-being of all citizens, and in the field of fiscal and monetary controls. There remains another area in which Americans long since have abandoned the rugged individualism of the past. That field is social welfare"* (Ellis, Harry B. *Ideal and Ideologies.* Cleveland: The World Publishing Co., 1968, p. 199).

Nowadays, nations can no longer say that they hold a neatly defined ideology. For example, most communist regimes are now introducing the profit incentive in their system while many capitalist countries have nationalized industries as well as many socialized systems. These three major ideologies, with all their imperfections, have one common goal: an improved life for all mankind.

I became involved politically when we received an anonymous threatening note stating that they were going to kidnap our children. On our arrival in San Francisco, we did not receive a warm welcome by some friends and members of our family. They were so impressed by the Sandinista Revolution that they just could not understand why we, as well as other professionals, had left the country. We told them that the leaders of the Sandinistas, whom my husband had known while attending the university, were communists. They would not believe us and argued with us. We decided not to discuss politics and told ourselves that time will tell the truth. After a few years, our friends and family turned against the Sandinistas because they revealed themselves for what they were.

I believe that it is difficult for communism to flourish in the USA climate where citizens have reverence for private property, equal political rights, and free education for rich and poor. In Latin America, poor uneducated people have no concept of the meaning of communism or democracy, nor are they particularly interested in finding out. They simply will support anyone who promises and delivers a better break in life as The *Communist Manifesto* says, *"The proletarians have nothing to lose but their chains. They have a world to win"* (Harold J. Laski on *The Communist Manifesto*_New York: Random House Inc., 1967, p. 179). Unfortunately, this is the only promise they are allowed to hear.

I used to get sad for the things I left behind in Nicaragua but no more. I must live in the present and for the future.

Principles have no real force except
when one is well-fed.

—Mark Twain

Esso, Chevron, University of San
Francisco and Colegio Teresiano

These are my memories of all the years
of hard work I accomplished in my
professional and educational journey.

Master of Science - University of San Francisco
December 20, 1997

Francisco, my husband, standing in the back. He had finished his first round of chemotherapy and radiation, and his hair was starting to grow back.

CHAPTER 11

My Professional and Educational Journey

I learned that there are no free lunches.
And I learned the value of hard work.
—Lee Iacocca

I left Esso in Nicaragua to start law school. My goal was to earn a degree in law at the Central American University (UCA) and join the law office of my husband and my father-in-law. UCA is a private Catholic Jesuit university. The school of law at this university offered a six-year program. In 1979, the political situation in my country was getting dangerous. The government imposed martial law. In spite of these problems, I continued to study as well as taking care of my family. Despite the political situation in 1979, I enrolled in my fourth year of law, but because things started to deteriorate, we decided to go on a three-week vacation to California with our four children: Ilean Reineri, Claudia Graciela, Deborah Linda, and Kattya Francis.

I left my relatives, I left my friends, I left Esso, I left the university, and I left my country.

After many required visits to the immigration office in California to renew my visa and to obtain residency papers, on September 15, 1980, I received my *green card*. It was that same day that I applied for a job at Standard Oil Company of California, now known as Chevron.

Chevron and the USA immigration office in San Francisco were located very close. Chevron was a beautiful historic building located on Bush Street and the USA immigration office located on Samsome Street. I asked my husband if we could go to Chevron to get an employment application form. I vividly remember this day. We owned a 1979 Ford Fairmont yellow station wagon. The red truck we brought from Nicaragua wasn't appropriate anymore for our big family.

On our way to Chevron, I was sitting in the front with my husband. In the back seat, Ilean Reineri was holding baby Lilette, Deborah in the middle, and Claudia holding Kattya. At this time, car seats and seat belts weren't enforced. My husband dropped me right in front of the building at 225 Bush Street. I went to the front desk and asked the receptionist for an employment application. As she proceeded giving me the application, she mentioned they were interviewing for two openings on the second floor; hence, I filled the application and rushed to the second floor. Great. The two open positions were junior typist and senior typist. These positions were ideal for me because I had good experience in typing, and this position didn't require face-to-face conversation. I wasn't fluent in English. There were seven candidates for these two positions.

The first test was spelling. We were allowed to miss of the list of words six words, and I missed five. So, I moved to the second test and at this time five of us. The category was punctuation. Again, we were allowed six mistakes, and I made five mistakes. Hence, I moved to the third test. At this time, it was only three of us going to the typing test. If you were able to type fifty-five words per minute, you would qualify as a junior typist, and sixty-five words per minute, you would qualify as a senior typist with a higher pay.

I closed my eyes and asked God to help me. It was a quick prayer and started typing. They gave us five minutes to warm up. I started typing, and fortunately, the typewriter was an IBM Selectric model, and I was familiar with it. I started typing nonstop. Well, I did not do sixty-five words per minute, but sixty-six words per minute. I just couldn't believe it. I've passed all the tests racing with people whose English was their first language.

After having passed the necessary tests, I went to the fifteenth floor for an interview. I totally forgot about my husband and my kids who were waiting for me outside on Bush Street. I couldn't miss this chance. At this point, my family needed the income from both of us so we would not deplete our savings. I met Pat Parker: blond, blue eyes, a very cute, and sweet lady. Pat was the human resources supervisor and in the same meeting was the lead of the typing pool, Lucy Stanovich. I felt from the very beginning of the interview that I had a good connection with Pat, but I didn't feel the same with Lucy, the lead. The interview went well, and Pat decided to give me the job even though Lucy mentioned that there were other candidates to be interviewed.

I got the senior typist job. I was on cloud nine. I was going to work for Chevron, a major organization, and while typing and getting paid, I was going to become fluent in English. I only had to take a few physical mandatory tests that I was sure I would pass. I'll never forget the date of this interview: September 15, 1980, which is the celebration of the Nicaraguan independence.

When I left the Chevron building, Francisco and my daughters were waiting for me. They had spent more than two hours waiting. Francisco thought I had left the building and that I had gotten lost. My oldest daughters looked at me upset, and the two little ones needed major diaper changes. Francisco wondered what had happened. I was supposed to just get an employment application. I told him very enthused, *"I got a job at Chevron as a senior typist with a salary of $1,200 a month."*

And he, in turn, said, *"What did you say?"*

And I responded, "That knowing my limitations in the language, I tried not to talk too much so they would not know I wasn't fluent in English, but I did smile a lot, and I tried to look confident and assertive. I also said the short speech I had memorized, and it worked!"

No doubt, God's favor was on my side that day! This was the beginning of a thirty-year journey with Chevron Corporation. I applied for a typing position because I felt unsure about adjusting to working in an all-English-speaking environment. I felt my English was not good enough to carry on a continuing dialogue all day. Any job is good to start a new life. I started working on October 6, 1980, for the personnel department.

Six months later, Lucy, my lead, approached me and said that my supervisor, Pat, wanted to talk to me. I immediately got frightened. But as always, I kept pretending I was confident even though from within I was shaking. I wondered, *Now they know I don't know anything.* I was sure I was going to be fired. Instead of going to her office, I went first to the restroom and started praying, *"Lord. Please. I don't want to be fired. I need this job. Please help me!"*

I walked into Pat's office just as cool and collected as possible. I said hello to her with a smile and sat across her desk. She reciprocated with a nice smile as well. Without wasting any time, she started saying that she had noticed I was overqualified for my job as a senior typist and that she had submitted my name for the office assistant position in the department of labor relations. I just couldn't believe it. I was not fired. I was promoted. Six months later, I was again promoted to lead office assistant in the same labor relation department.

As lead office assistant, I continued acquiring experience. I provided support to the labor relation counselors as well as handling union-related confidential material. I was fortunate to work in this department because through it, I could say that every day I kept adding many new terms to my vocabulary and gained a better understanding of the interrelationships within a huge corporation.

I was blessed with a wonderful department head, Ed Johannessen, and a loving but strict supervisor, Connie Jones. The department head had been working for Standard Oil Company of California for many years. He was a well-educated, a well-read intellectual, neat, and extremely conservative running a tight operation, but human-oriented. He cared about the people who worked for him.

I resented that I had to interrupt my law studies in Nicaragua. I had the desire to go back to school. But how? When? Where? Sometime later, I learned that Chevron had an educational refund program, and I immediately started researching that possibility. I also heard about the University of San Francisco (USF). This was a Jesuit University, and my studies in Nicaragua were also from a Jesuit University. So, I started dreaming.

I know that if you have a dream, and you set a deadline, your dream might come true. I called my mother in Nicaragua and asked her to get from the university all my academic records with all the courses I had taken as well as all grades received and to accordingly legalize the entire transcripts and to make sure to include in the certification process the American Embassy in Managua. I, of course, had the support from Francisco to go back to school. I was admitted at USF and started night school. In 1985, my youngest daughter, Lilette, graduated from kinder, and I graduated as well. I received a Bachelor of Science in organizational behavior. Because of my previous studies in Nicaragua, I was able to obtain a bachelor's degree in eighteen months.

My supervisor, Connie Jones, was kind and encouraging from the minute I started reporting to her. She was instrumental in teaching me how to handle my time, my coworkers, make decisions, set priorities, and how to multitask. I had felt at times that it would be so wonderful to be able to grow two more arms in order to do six things at a time.

Not being content with just a bachelor's degree, after a break, I went back to school to obtain a master's degree in organizational behavior including a thesis in leadership styles. Now, again, when Lilette graduated from high school, I also graduated. I received the degree of Master of Science in human resources and organizational development from the college of professional studies at USF.

My continuous education helped me advance in the company obtaining promotions such as human resources assistant and eventually as human resources business partner with Chevron Shipping, Chevron Real Estate, Chevron Aircraft, Chevron Procurement, and Chevron Corporation.

One of USF's prerequisite to obtain a master's degree was to submit a research study/thesis. I presented a research study centered on leadership styles within Chevron Real Estate Management Company.

The thesis background was to determine whether the leadership style correlated with job satisfaction. Also, to learn about the leadership behaviors and the impact on subordinates' job satisfaction. *The expectations* were to point to ways of continuing or improving effective behaviors as well as eliminating behaviors not effective. *The variables* consisted of leaders, subordinates, transformation leadership style, transactional leadership style, and job satisfaction.

I based this research on two hypotheses. *Hypothesis one*: a proposed explanation of the leadership style using the score on the Multifactor Leadership Questionnaire (MLQ) that *transformational* and *transactional* styles influence subordinates' job satisfaction. Hypothesis two: that subordinates working under a transformational leader will report higher job satisfaction than will individuals working under a transactional leader.

Through this study, it was important for leaders to gain a better understanding of her or his own style and group's reaction and become aware of alternative behaviors. Chevron management supported this research. Under this study, there were some limitations: honesty and candor, downsizing, reorganizing, level of perceived threat, motivation, and self-esteem.

To handle this project, I researched and reviewed literature written on leader, subordinate, models of leadership styles, transformational, and transactional styles. The methodology included subjects/ participants, research design, instrumentation, procedure, operational definition of relevant variables, and treatment of data. In the research design, this study utilized leadership team members and subordinates. The variables studied consisted of leadership styles, transformational, and transactional and job satisfaction. The instrumentation utilized was the Bass's Multifactor Leadership Questionnaire (MLQ). This tool was used to measure subordinates' perceptions of transformational and transactional leadership. The questionnaire consisted of transformational leadership, transactional leadership, and non-leadership. As well as a Job Satisfaction Questionnaire (JSQ) to measure subordinates' job satisfaction. I worked with two excellent advisors from USF.

Attending USF was a major challenge. Those were busy and difficult days, but God kept showing up with blessings. I remember I went to visit Alba, my hairdresser, to have a haircut. Alba noticed a big round bald spot in the back of my head. The round bald spot was of approximately two inches. I went to see the doctor, and he mentioned two possible causes: alopecia or stress. He described alopecia as a sudden hair loss that starts with circular bald spots and that is incurable, or that it could be stress caused by mental emotional tension. I was taking care of my family, taking care of my husband, who was fighting cancer, and I was working full time at Chevron.

I continued praying and meditating. Our God is our vindicator. We must keep the faith. It is through fire that we are made stronger. I found out early in life that if you persevere, you will attain what you seek. Although I had a large family to take care of and job responsibilities, I knew that if I worked hard enough, I would reach my objective. Once I reached a goal, I knew there will be many more the challenge is there, and I was ready to meet it. The good Lord continued to watch over my family and me. And, by the way, the bald spot went away.

After many years with Chevron, I left the company on March 30, 2000, due to my husband's terminal illness. Six months later, Chevron called me back to assist during the Texaco acquisition.

I had loved every second working for Chevron and the wonderful people I met and developed long-term friendships and memories. I will always be thankful to Chevron and many of the people I met for having given me opportunity to not only develop my own skills but to contribute my passion and love to the human resources function and continuous improvement Chevron's philosophy over the many years. I couldn't ask for anything more than to work for a company that I am so very proud of and to be able to go to work every day and really enjoy what I did and the many different managers/supervisors I worked with.

I learned so much while at Chevron including becoming fluent in English. At Chevron, it is ingrained in our minds, as we work, to walk our talk; and we, all including contractors, really care about safety, the environment, and the health and safety of coworkers so that employees and contractors could go home safe to their families.

Anytime I would get nervous, I would pray, and it totally helped. I worked super hard, but when you love what you are doing, working hard is not even noticed. At some point when I was at the level of giving presentations as a human resources business partner in front of a group, I would practice in front of my oldest daughters, and they would say, *"You are good! You sound great!"* Later, I would practice in front of my two youngest daughters. It was so different. First, they both laughed at my accent, and they and I will laugh a lot; but later, we got serious, and they would correct my pronunciation.

During my employment with Chevron, I obtained a Bachelor of Science degree and a Master of Science degree, but Chevron was the leading university where I perfected English and forced me to grow intellectually. Little by little, my analytical skills got better and better. My English communication and my writing skills improved every day. I experienced an enormous amount of learning every day. I dealt with supervisors with huge hearts, great mentors, and incredible role models.

While working in human resources, I interacted with high-level executives as well as with the janitorial staff. I honestly can say I obtained an enormous experience. It is great when you know you don't know, but you are willing to take a risk and learn. I always kept my eyes open for opportunities. I never expected to go through all these wonderful exiting things in my life: A Mom, a wife, working for one of the largest oil company in the world, and attending the university. Two important things I learned at Chevron: safety and continuous improvement. My learning curve wasn't curved, it was vertical. I am a firm believer that education doesn't stop at graduation. It is a lifelong journey.

As soon as I was hired by Chevron, I realized I loved it. Even though I faced many challenges, I never faced any kind of discrimination, or any kind of harassment. I was given a lot of opportunities. In many occasions, I took on a project I didn't feel ready to do, but I still worked on it and that's when I stretched, I grew, and I learned. In a few words, I can say I was super lucky at Chevron. Chevron always treated me with respect. I met so many people and learned how to deal with so many different individuals: people that looked different from me and people with different perspectives.

Chevron became my second home, and it was a refuge after the loss of my husband. Unfortunately, when I retired, I wasn't able to enjoy it with my husband. My husband's life was cut short, but he went to heaven with the satisfaction that he left us in a safe place.

God turned the heart of those around me. When you honor God, even your enemies will shake your hand.

Once you stop learning you start dying.
—Albert Einstein

Ilean and Her
Five Treasures

From left to right: Lilette, Ilean R., Kattya, Me, Deborah, and Claudia.

CHAPTER 12

UC Berkeley Mom

*If you are planning for a year, sow rice; if you
are planning for a decade, plant trees; if you
are planning for a lifetime, educate people.*
—Chinese proverb

Motherhood is a priceless gift from God. Moments of quiet are very scarce. God entrusted me with five treasures. This chapter might show a little bit of bragging, but parents are allowed to brag about their children. My husband wanted to have boys and girls. He even had the name ready for the boy every time I got pregnant: *Francisco Ernesto Baltodano III*. Instead of a boy, we ended up having five beautiful and successful daughters. Every time we had another girl, he would say, "*Who wants a boy?*"

Every time someone would say, "*Your daughters are beautiful!*"

He would immediately respond, "*I made them all by myself.* Ha! Ha!"

When we arrived in the USA, with children so young not even teenagers, I felt fear, and I was faced with a major challenge. I would ask my Lord to tell me where to go and how to get there. The feeling of vulnerability is hard to describe. Migrating to another country is definitely life changing. Coming on vacation to this country with empty suitcases and eventually forced to stay was a tremendous decision and a challenge. I currently have a big family: five daughters, four sons-in-law, and eleven grandchildren (four granddaughters and seven grandsons).

Thank God my daughters didn't go through the experience thousands of children have to go through to find their mothers in the United States. Some of those children and families travel a much scarier journey, such as *The Beast* also known as *The Train of Death*. Hundreds of migrants ride on top of this train heading north. They make this horrible decision looking for freedom. The new immigration laws are forcing immigrants into new scary journeys.

I am so grateful I didn't leave my children behind, but obviously, I had to take them out of my country after an anonymous threatening note we received hoping we would be gone just for a short time. Although I was naive to think I was coming to USA just for a three-week vacation. While I didn't arrive illegally, nor I didn't travel on top of a train, I experienced fear. It is challenging bringing up a family of five daughters in a foreign country.

My daughters were forced to mature and look after themselves at a young age. As sisters growing up, they argued, they fussed, they fought, they loved, and they stuck together. Obviously, being part of a big family has its advantages and disadvantages. We moved to a country where our kids were able to develop their God-given talents by working hard.

My girls have been empowered in the environment of the United States of America. I remember when I was told that I couldn't make it in this country with five children. She said, "*How many kids do you have? One, two, three, four, five?"* She continued saying, *"There is no way you will be able to survive or succeed in this country. You are used to help in Nicaragua. You should go back."* I didn't respond to her comments. Obviously, going back was not an option; hence, we were determined to survive and to succeed including our young daughters as they noticed our struggles. She was wrong! We made it! That wasn't my faith. That was the faith of God. If your faith is low, the faith of God is high.

I came to this country in 1979. I am sharing my story to encourage immigrant families and their children. *¡Que sí se puede! (Yes, you can!).* Don't let anyone tell you, you cannot do it. Even though we don't live in a fairy-tale world, the sky is the limit, and anything is possible if you work hard.

My daughters are making a difference in this country. My daughters are an asset to this country. They were trained that if they were willing to work hard, they could do and could be anything they wanted to be. They give me great pride. They worked jobs while going to college/university because they needed the income, because work is a learning experience, and because work dignifies.

I am a UC Berkeley Mom! All five of my daughters are CAL alumni. The University of California, Berkeley, is a research university located in Berkeley, California. The University of California, Berkeley, is also referred to as just Berkeley, UC Berkeley, or CAL. It was founded in 1868. It is often cited as the top public university in the United States and around the world. Even though CAL is a public university, CAL is not free. I hope sometime in the near future, students would be able to graduate from college debt free.

Allow me to brag a little.

Ilean Reineri has a double major in history and political science, a Juris Doctor (JD) degree, a master's in tax law from Georgetown University. She passed the California bar examination.

Claudia has a major in architecture and a major in computer science.

Deborah has a double major in electrical engineering and computer science.

Kattya has a major in linguistics.

Lilette Jill has a major in political science. She obtained a Juris Doctor (JD) degree and passed the California bar examination.

My daughters are exceptional not for what they have done but because they are my children no matter what. Even though we didn't come with wealth, we came with a spirit of dignity and respect. Furthermore, love and education start with the family. It is criminal to separate families and to disconnect these two elements.

God has blessed me with a loving family. Family is a priceless gift.

Here is a tribute to my daughters:

Forever Young Lyrics
Rod Stewart

May the good Lord be with you
down every road you roam
And may sunshine and happiness surround
you when you're far from home
And may you grow to be proud, dignified, and true
And do unto others as you'd have done to you
Be courageous and be brave
And in my heart, you'll always stay
Forever young

May good fortune be with you, may
your guiding light be strong
Build a stairway to heaven with
a prince or a vagabond
And may you never love in vain
And in my heart you will remain
Forever young

And when you'll finally fly away, I'll
be hoping that I served you well
For all the wisdom of a lifetime, no one can ever tell
But whatever road you choose, I'm
right behind you, win or lose
Forever young

CHAPTER 13

A Tourist in My Country

It does not matter how slowly you go
as long as you do not stop.

—Confucius

In 2012, thirty-two years later, I flew to visit my homeland Nicaragua. It's incredible what has happened to my identity. In USA, I am a Latina/Hispanic, and when I went to my country, they didn't believe I was Nicaraguan. I'm so proud when I say Nicaragua is beautiful and is the largest of the Central American countries. But in reality, Nicaragua is just a grain of mustard compared to other countries. But as our Nicaraguan poet Ruben Darío said, *"If the homeland is small, you dream of it big." (Si pequeña es la Patria, uno grande la sueña.)*

It was Wednesday, May 30, 2012. I came to stay overnight with Claudia, my daughter. She lives in San Bruno, which is fifteen minutes away from the San Francisco Airport. I decided to stay in San Bruno to avoid the morning traffic coming from Benicia, which is where I live.

I see the rays of light coming through the windows, and the alarm from my iPhone just went off. It is 5:00 a.m. on Thursday, May 31, 2012. It is time for me to get ready for my trip which is four thousand miles away. Benicia is located thirty-five miles northeast of San Francisco. My daughter's house is the first house we bought in 1980 when we decided we were not going back to Nicaragua. This house is located on top of a hill. It has a picturesque vista.

Just to give you an idea, San Bruno offers attractive hiking opportunities with lovely views. Birds are quite common and widespread, especially birds of prey. The rodents' population is diverse. In fact, there is a major raccoon plague as well as rats.

Now, let's go back to my trip. I'm ready to travel. I've decided to visit my country. I am leaving for Managua, Nicaragua. It sounds incredible that time has gone by so fast. My family and I left Managua in June 1979 on a three-week vacation. This vacation has already lasted too many years.

It is 9:00 a.m. Claudia is giving me a ride to the San Francisco Airport. I am in line going through all the safety requirements before boarding. As many of you know, since September 11, 2001, attacks, flight inspections are stricter. Airport and airlines security measures are in place to prevent terrorism in order to protect air passengers and crew. I went through the inspection without any difficulties. Now, I'm heading toward my designated gate to go to Houston, Texas, my first stop. Thus far, I have to admit I am in denial. I feel I am just traveling to a country I haven't visited. A land simply as when I traveled to Africa, Turkey, or even Romania.

It is now 11:20 a.m. I'm heading to Houston, Texas. This flight will last approximately three hours and forty-two minutes. I'm trying to record some of the activities of my journey, but in turn, I have decided to take a nap.

Flight attendants offered a variety of beverages but no special meal. Meals were just available for purchase. I packed a few snacks: crackers, almonds, and raisins. The flight went practically fast.

Time goes by so fast. It is now 7:02 p.m. in Houston, Texas. We are boarding United Airlines 1421 to arrive Managua, Nicaragua, at 9:22 p.m. This flight will last approximately two hours and twenty minutes. Now, I'm getting emotional. I will be arriving soon to Managua, Nicaragua. Every minute that goes by takes me closer and closer to my destination.

When I started this trip, I tried to document with a recorder all the details of this journey. But it didn't work for me. I preferred using pen and paper. Handwriting could probably be a slower process, but in this manner, I feel that my head and heart are connected with my hand and my hand with the pen and paper.

I'm flying to Managua, Nicaragua, from my California home. I will be arriving late in the evening. I am getting ready to say hello to my dear Managua.

It is around 9:45 p.m. We are now landing at the Managua Airport. We've already followed the flight attendant instructions to fasten seat belt and sit upright. The landing is somewhat abrupt.

We are leaving the aircraft. Our first stop is with immigration. They all have khaki uniforms, and they don't seem to be busy at this late time of the evening. A male guy checked my USA passport; no problem at all. He was courteous and asked me if I was North American. I explained to him that I was Nicaraguan but that I had been gone for quite some time.

Now, I'm ready to leave the airport building. I don't have a luggage to pick up. I just brought a hand carry bag for the few days I will be staying in Managua. They let me go without checking my hand carry bag.

It's dark, and the weather is warm and humid outside the Managua airport building. I'm looking for the hotel taxi driver. The walkway and the street are wet, but it is not raining anymore. There is a long line of taxicabs. I see that there is a taxi driver holding up high a long rectangular white sign showing my name: *Ilean Baltodano*.

It is around 10:15 p.m., and I am inside the taxi. The driver works for the hotel I will be staying: The Real InterContinental, Metrocentro, Managua.

It is noticeable that it has been raining, and the taxi driver confirms it. The streets are wet and black. The roads are covered with paving stones instead of asphalt. This type of cement blocks are called in Spanish Adoquín, which translates as paving stone, or paving block. The only inconvenience, as the driver explained to me, is that because the rain has been so heavy, it has been lifting these bricks. Even though it is so dark and there is not good illumination, I can see mud everywhere. The temperature is approximately 90 degrees Fahrenheit. During this month of August, the most common forms of precipitation are thunderstorms and drizzle. Humidity typically ranges from 56 percent (mildly humid) to 96 percent (very humid).

As we drive to the hotel, the driver is pointing out the names of some of the buildings, such as Coca Cola and Milk buildings, and others I don't remember because I was getting a little tired.

I am now walking toward the hotel. As I approach the main door, I am welcomed and directed to the front desk. The hotel employees appeared to be very well trained. They are polite and friendly. After signing all the necessary papers, I am ready to go to my room. I'm so tired.

I have been assigned to the sixth floor. A guy is helping me with my luggage and directing me to the elevator and the floor where I have been assigned to room 619. I will also have access, through a special card key, to the eighth executive floor where I could have breakfast from 6:00 a.m. to 10:00 p.m. and happy hour from 6:00 p.m. to 8:00 p.m. In this way, I don't have to go down the first floor for breakfast. Oh well, I cannot complain. God is good!

It is almost midnight. I sit quietly by my bed. Before I went to bed, I unpacked so that tomorrow, everything will be in order, and I will be ready to go out. As I am unpacking, I am realizing that I'm in Nicaragua, and at this moment, I'm just humbled. I'm filled with appreciation as how life and God has treated me. I'm ready to go to bed, but because I am so tired, I am not able to fall sleep. On top of that, I have a major headache. Good. It went away.

At this point, I got inspired and motivated to write. The paving stones and the mud while driving from the airport to the hotel are still in my mind. I wrote the following that goes like this:

The Paving Stones Speak Up in Nicaragua
Ilean Baltodano

Paving stones here
Paving stones everywhere
Piled paving stones
Lonesome broken paving stones

What are they trying to say?
How can I understand their language?
Do they also feel the pressure?
How is it possible? They are only paving stones

Holes here
Holes everywhere
Piles of dirt
Mud everywhere

The paving stones do not want to be buried
The paving stones want to be free
The paving stones are rebelling
What can we learn from them?

The rain is their exhaust
The rain is their freedom
Blessed waters of May!
Bring liberation to the stones and your people!

I woke up early this morning. This is my first full day in Managua. I will be meeting around 9:00 a.m. with my tour guy. I will start my day by enjoying a good Nicaraguan breakfast. I'm going to the eighth floor.

I have so many things going in my mind. I just want to ask a few questions to myself. Perhaps to reinforce myself on what should I do or shouldn't do. I have been gone for thirty-three years. I left Nicaragua in 1979 on a three-week vacation that has lasted thirty-three years so far. I'm truly wondering what I am doing in Nicaragua at this time of my life and by myself. I am looking for a lost love. Nicaragua is my lost love.

As an introvert, I am focused more on internal thoughts rather than seeking out external stimulation. I enjoy thinking a lot. In other words, be on my own. Even though I'm not a professional writer, much less in English as my second language, I enjoy writing. I just feel that I have to write down my emotions, excitements, enthusiasm, or indifference. This is also hard for me, but with practice, I will eventually master it. Many times, I ask myself, "How come I am not an ordinary person just doing ordinary things?" Why writing and lonely whether in USA or Managua, Nicaragua? I need to know. What is my identity? Is it what people choose that I am, or is it going to be what I feel I am? Perhaps are both because it is out of my control what people think who I am. It is under my control what I believe I am. Maybe it will be both. I am Nicaraguan with USA citizenship. No question about it. Which one is my country? They are both my countries. The only odd thing I've noticed is that I try to communicate in English while in Managua and in Spanish while in USA.

I'm ready to go to the eighth floor to have breakfast. It's 8:00 a.m., Friday, and the day is just starting. I'm watching people through the many windows of the breakfast area in the hotel. Many people are rushing, and I'm assuming they are going to work. Some are catching a bus or a minivan. Others must be waiting for a ride. I see through the window men, women, and children. Riding bikes, motorcycles, or walking in different directions carrying backpacks, other purses, and some brown paper bags.

I better go serve my breakfast. Breakfast on the eighth floor opens at 6:00 a.m. and is for VIPs. But I am not a VIP. Oh well, I am on the eighth floor. It is, of course, better than continental breakfast. The service and the quality of the food are outstanding. White porcelain serving dishes full of a variety of cereals. Trays are full with delicious pastry as well as French and sour bread. Plates are full of lively multicolored tropical fruits: watermelon, pineapple, banana, papaya, orange, and zapote.

This tropical fruit zapote is believed to have been derived from the Aztec tzapotl. This fruit is round and sometimes elliptic from three to nine inches long and ranges in weight from half a pound to five pounds. It has rough dark-brown skin and salmon-pink to deep-red soft flesh, sweet and pumpkin-like in flavor and a single large seed. This fruit is called in English marmalade or natural marmalade. It is delicious. For many years, I haven't had zapote fruit.

They also serve apples, pears, strawberries, and grapes. Fruits are cut in different shapes and sizes: square, rectangular, round, small, medium, and large. They serve all different kinds of pastry, and of course, a variety of Nicaraguan foods, such as gallo pinto, which is rice mixed with red beans.

Plantains, either ripe or green, are delicious. Plantains resemble green bananas, and they are a member of the banana family. They are starchy and cooked before serving, green or ripe typically fried or baked. Plantains are somewhat like a potato.

They also serve eggs cooked in different styles: fried, hard boiled, soft boiled, and scrambled. You will find a variety of tasty vegetables and many more dishes. The breakfast area is designed with fine furniture and paintings. The atmosphere is a full-service style. They invite you to be seated at the table. I would describe this breakfast area as a fine-casual atmosphere.

While watching people through the window on the eighth floor of the hotel, those walking on the streets appear to me as if they are dancing in slow motion. I also see people riding in trucks to an unknown destination from my point of view. I see others in bikes and bicycles. I see bright colors everywhere. The paint in most homes is bright and colorful: bright yellow, brick red, and mustard, just like the mustard we spread in a hamburger. I also see a lot of dark brown. Not sure if it's dark due to the mud of all the rain that has been falling down lately. The majority of people on the streets are also dressed in bright vibrant colors.

I'm going back to my room and get ready to go out not knowing what I will come across. I will be trying to capture all the reality around me: the warm air, the smell of wet soil, the people, the roads, associating how things were in the past and how they are now. No judgment how things are now. I'm just humbled. I'm filled with appreciation as how life and God has treated me.

I hired a driver/tour guide who was a very polite person. I met him through Claudia, my daughter. Claudia visits Nicaragua on mission trips with volunteers. At this moment, is interesting according to my perception, I feel I am visiting new places, not the Managua I used to know. Everything seems different to me. The city has changed, and it has expanded into areas that were green areas before. One thing that hasn't change and will not change is the weather. It is warm and humid. This humidity makes my hair frizzy, but there is nothing I can do. I see many smiling faces and friendly people as if they are saying, "*Welcome!*"

I'm ready to go out with Joel, the tour guide. Before I get in the car, I observe the brightness of the sun and feel the warm humid weather. It feels good. So, I decided to walk just for five minutes before getting in the car. I noticed that people look at me with a friendly smile. But I noticed, they treat me as a foreigner. Two individuals asked me if I was North American. I, of course, responded, "*No, I'm Nicaraguan who has been away for quite some time.*" I said, "*I'm back for just a few days, but I will return.*" As Joel starts driving in different areas, I hardly recognize anything because almost everything has either moved or changed, and it looks different. When I lived in Nicaragua, Managua was centralized toward the Lake of Managua. After the major earthquake in 1972, the old Managua was not rebuilt, and businesses were forced to move in other areas which forced Managua to be more decentralized.

According to Wikipedia Encyclopedia:

> *The population of Nicaragua is approximately 6 million and it is multiethnic. Roughly a quarter of the population lives in the capital city, Managua. It is the second-largest city in Central America. Segments of the population include indigenous native tribes from the Mosquito Coast, Europeans, Africans, Asians, and people of Middle Eastern origin. The main language is Spanish, although native tribes on the eastern coast speak their native languages, such as Miskito, Sumo, and Rama, as well as English Creole. The mixture of cultural traditions has generated substantial diversity in art and literature, particularly the latter given the various literary contributions of Nicaraguan writers, including Ruben Dario, Ernesto Cardenal and Gioconda Belli.*

I *must* include in this memoir a poem from Ruben Dario. He is considered the father of the modernism movement. Here is the English version of the poem. Though, in my opinion, it sounds better in its original Spanish version.

Fatal
Rubén Darío, 1905

Blessed is the tree for it can hardly feel
And even more the stone, because it feels
no more,
For there is no greater pain than the pain of
living or greater grief than life with
conscious thought.
To be and to not know, and without a
course to be, and the fear of having been
and the terror the future holds.
And the sure fright that tomorrow death
will find me and to suffer life, and to bear
the shadow, and to suffer for
That which we do not know and can hardly
guess
and the temptations of the fresh fruits of
flesh and the tomb awaits with wreaths
of internment
and to not know where we're going next
or where we surfaced...

On Saturday evening, while at the hotel, there was a big wedding celebration. I went closer and started talking to people to find out who was getting married. It happened that I was talking to two ladies who happened to be the bride's aunts. They were friendly, and they even invited me to the wedding. Of course, I nicely declined the invitation but stayed to take a few pictures of the beautiful bride and handsome groom. I've been taking pictures everywhere. I've been careful at not losing anything: camera, wallet, glasses, passport, recorder, and money. I've been giving tips generously, and it has given me satisfaction when I see the gratefulness in people's faces.

It is Sunday. I am now alone by choice in my country, Nicaragua. Everybody is expecting something out of this trip. I'm trying to do so many things at once in such a short time: recording, taking pictures,

111

writing, reading, listening, watching, eating, and sleeping. I feel I've covered what I wanted to visit. I really enjoyed my stay.

I've just noticed I haven't had any allergies. I guess it's because I am now surrounded by natural elements. I just realized I haven't needed my lubricating eye drops. My eyes have not been drying at all. I'm in my bedroom. Even though I'm by myself, I'm not lonely. In fact, I feel I needed this time. When I arrived, I immediately started unpacking, but now, I'm getting ready to leave very early tomorrow, and I'm starting to pack.

It is hard to believe that I came back to Nicaragua after thirty-three years. I haven't mentioned that I purposely traveled to look for those individuals who in my youth tried to sexually abuse me. My plan was to meet them, to deal with my feelings, and be able to move on. I was not able to confront them because they both had died. I decided I was going to forget them and forgive them.

When I left Nicaragua in 1979, it seemed pretty big. Now it looks pretty small. Did it change, or did I change? Another thing I noticed is that the majority of the roads in Nicaragua have new names. Joel is a fine young tour guide. He knows the old names and the new names of the roads, and it helps me correlate them. I realized Joel's young age and wondered how he knew the old names of the streets. He mentioned that his grandfather taught him the old names and that it has helped him in his role as a tour guide.

Given that I was going to be in Nicaragua for such a short time, I tried to capture all the reality around me. Associating how things were in the past and how they are now. I tried not to judge how things are now, but I just could not. I was just humbled and filled with appreciation as how life and God has treated me.

Of course, my stay in Nicaragua moved me. This visit to Nicaragua was a humble and emotional experience: the warm air, the smell of wet soil, and the friendly people with their big smiles. To be honest, I was offended by the huge metal trees all around the city of Managua. The metal trees, more of 140 of them. These are electrical tall sculptures of fifty-six feet known as the *tree of life*. These expensive sculptures require costly maintenance. They adorn parks and street corners. Nicaragua is a poor country. I got inspired and wrote the following:

Metallic Trees in Nicaragua
Ilean Baltodano

What has happened to my beautiful Nicaragua?
Metallic trees
Artificial trees; trees out of metal
This is a sad vision!

This vision paints a titanic sadness
This oppressive government has replaced you
Only fools build trees out of metal
Only God almighty can create you

The tree of life?
No! These are dead trees
Trees without roots, without leaves, unscented
Trees without sap, lifeless trees
Dear tree, the birds and Nicaragua—they need you

For heaven's sake!
You are a refuge to the birds
You provide shadow to the tired walker
You provide fruits and clean the air
You provide wood without question

You will return to brighten Managua
You don't need electric power
You will replace the metal trees
You are the tree of life
There is hope for you and Nicaragua

I also decided to ask Joel if he was happy with the Sandinista government. His response was quick and honest. *"This is all I have known."*

I felt the desire that time would have stood still. I had so much to see and people to meet after so many years. It is Monday, June 4, and it is four in the morning. I see the rays of light coming through the window right through the side of my bed. I just received a wakeup call. I'm getting ready to take a hotel car to the airport. It is time for me to get ready for my trip back to USA. San Francisco is four thousand miles away from Managua, Nicaragua. My daughter will pick me up. I'm going home!

CHAPTER 14

Life Goes On

In Autumn
(fragment)
Rubén Darío

I know there are those who ask:
Why does he not sing with the same
wild harmonies as before?
But they have not seen the labors of an hour,
The work of a minute,
The prodigies of a year.
I am an aged tree that, when I was
growing uttered a vague, sweet
sound when the breeze caressed me.
The time for youthful smiles has now passed by

This vacation has been a long journey. I question again. Why is it that when your life is moving on so well, all of a sudden, something happens? Why is it that when you get sick or encounter a problem, you suddenly love waking up and you suddenly love a sunset? You love breathing. I guess we shouldn't take anything for granted.

My husband was a 6'4" tall and 225-pound man. Good guy. At an early age of fifty-three, my husband was diagnosed with sarcoma of the soft tissue located in his abdominal area. It was devastating. We had so many plans after retirement. He would see old couples, and he would say, "*We are going to look like those couples.*" The diagnostic of sarcoma of the soft tissue in his abdominal area was a major surprise. He was such a healthy person.

I remember receiving a long distance call from Nicaragua. Mom called very emotional even crying to let me know that she had a dental problem. Her upper teeth would have to be removed. In other words, she would have to get an upper denture. Of course, I was sad and sorry, but how can I convince her that there are worse situations? "*Mom,*" I said, "*You have a solution, and who cares if you need to wear a denture. No one needs to know.*" I went on saying, "*I have bad news for you. Francisco has been diagnosed with cancer located in the abdominal area. Pray for Francisco, Mom.*"

They ran several tests to determine why his right leg was swollen. The tests revealed a mass in his right side of his lower abdominal area. My work at Chevron was moving in the right direction. I was, as always, busy but happy. I didn't know that the health situation of my husband would impact my career.

To be able to remove the tumor in the abdominal area, he underwent three major surgeries in a period of three exhausting years. It was so much to absorb. According to tests, what he had was sarcoma of the soft tissue malignant, but fortunately, it had not spread, but eventually, it did.

To educate myself about my husband's illness, I started reading more about cancer, chemo therapy, and motivational books. I didn't want to admit that I was going to be left alone with five daughters. That I had to start doing all kinds of new things that he was doing. Even though I had a driver's license, I wasn't driving. I was not even doing grocery shopping on my own. I would go with him. The two most painful things after he passed away were going shopping and going to church.

At the hospital, before his first surgery we all six, my five daughters and myself, were having so much fun as to how he looked wearing a white gown and a bonnet on his head. We might have been in denial, but we tried to have fun. The nurse came and said with a big smile, "*Hey, this is not a party, nor happy hour.*" We all laughed and tried to be quiet but hoping everything would be okay, as always.

On this surgery, he had a portion of his stomach removed, and a big portion of the aorta, the main artery of the body, through a bypass, and a portion of his large intestine removed. After the surgery, I said, "*You did it, chiquito. I'm so glad the mass was contained.*" He used to call me chiquita, which means "little," and it's okay because I am only 5'2". In turn, I called him chiquito.

His surgeon and oncologist were so positive, compassionate, and the finest doctors to treat his illness. The surgeon, a very handsome guy, told my husband, "Francisco, you should be a movie star in Hollywood." And that comment made my husband feel like a million-dollar guy.

On his second procedure, he underwent a major surgery. The surgeon removed a portion of three major organs: stomach, pancreas and large intestine. The surgery took over ten hours. After ten hours, the surgeon couldn't attach the intestine. Hence, he left him with a plastic bag called ileostomy. We didn't tell anyone, but every night I was waking up constantly because one time, the bag was so full that we both got full of poo; but you know what, you don't care when you're taking care of your loved one. True love always loves through health and through illness. Anytime I would ask him how he was doing, he would say, "*We are going to be all right. Don't you worry.*" He was physically and spiritually incredibly strong. He would recover fast every time he underwent surgery. I don't know how he was able to handle bad news. He was always so positive and confident.

I loved my husband, and if you would have known him, you would have loved him too. I want to be like him (sobbing). As I mentioned earlier, he said about his daughters, very proud, that they all looked like him and that he made them all by himself. Ha. Ha.

Of course, we always hoped cancer would go away, but unfortunately this cancer, sarcoma of the soft tissue, kept spreading in his abdominal area. Six months later after his third surgery, they removed the ileostomy (the bag) and attached his intestine.

In November, during Thanksgiving of 1999, his cancer came back, but the doctor didn't call me until after the holiday. The doctor indicated he could not cut any more organs.

I asked the doctor, "*How long can we expect?*"

And he wisely responded, "*Only God knows.*"

Since then, he started to noticeably become weaker and weaker. He was physically debilitated. What doctors had originally said was that sarcoma of the soft tissue commonly spreads. The 6'4" tall handsome guy and 230 pounds wasn't anymore, but I didn't care. I loved him even more.

At this point, he needed me full time. I requested a family leave of absence from work. In January 2000, he started hospice and pain medication. I didn't know anything about hospice. Hospice is a home providing care for the sick or terminally ill. In every fairy tale, you want to ideally end your story with the quote "*And they lived happily ever after.*" That wasn't our case.

One day, my husband was my support, my pillar; and the next day, I became his support, his pillar, making most of the major decisions. And suddenly, all our future dreams evaporated. My daughters, my father-in-law, and I were all around him while he was lying in bed dying. He passed away on January 26, 2000.

> *I have fought the good fight,*
> *I have finished the race,*
> *I have kept the faith.*
> —2 Timothy 4:7

The End of the World
Brenda Lee

Why does the sun go on shining
Why does the sea rush to shore
Don't they know it's the end of the world
'Cause you don't love me anymore, YES

Why do the birds go on singing
Why do the stars glow above
Don't they know it's the end of the world
It ended when I lost your love

I wake up in the mornin' and I wonder
Why everything's the same as it was
I can't understand, NO
I can't understand
How life goes on the way it does

Why does my heart go on beating
Why do these eyes of mine cry
Don't they know it's the end of the world
I ended when you said goodbye
Goodbye!
(When you went to heaven!)

Losing your companion is the most horrible thing that can happen to a family, and it happened to my five daughters and me. Even though losing someone is a universal reality that we all will go through now or later, we'll never accept it as a normal event. I will never understand why God allowed my husband's early death, but nothing will keep me from trusting God because God knows what he is doing. I didn't know how I would end, but I kept moving forward. Anything friends would say to comfort me would ring hollow. Yet I never lost control. I kept saying to myself, "I'm going to be okay in spite of my big loss." What did I have left? Of course, we had each other: my five daughters and good friends.

In October 2000, the call from Chevron to assist with the acquisition of Texaco was a blessing. Work became my safe haven. No doubt that life is unpredictable. Many times, I felt afraid in my new world. Again, life is unpredictable and fragile. I decided to take one breath and one heartbeat at a time. I have no idea how my five daughters were able to support this major ordeal. In May, four months later, my daughter Ilean Reineri had her first baby, my first grandchild, Gabriella. God is good! What a challenge and a mock: one life fading away while a new life appears to give us so much joy— my first granddaughter.

My husband was such a healthy person that I depended on him even to go grocery shopping, driving, going to church, paying bills, and of course, making major decisions. Suddenly, he turns into a husband and father confronting his own mortality. Francisco, also known by most by his nickname, Chico, was an attorney named after his Dad who was an attorney as well. Chico grew up in California, and returned to Nicaragua after he graduated from high school. He graduated from law school in Nicaragua from the Universidad Centro Americana. When I met him, I said to myself, "*That's the man I'm going to marry.*" It was love at first sight.

The year 2000 was a challenging year in my life. Losing Francisco was very painful and forced me to readjust my life and to reshape myself within. I was able to find peace in books, friends, daughters, and in my new first granddaughter, Gabriella. The three days that I took care of her were the highlight of my week. It was such a great joy to see her smile and to be with her as she was growing up.

I stopped working when my husband became ill and subsequently passed away. Six months later, Chevron called me back, and I accepted the job offer but to work part time. The days at work gave me great purpose, fulfillment, and happiness. Being a stay-at-home mom is not for me, and this has nothing to do with any feminist movement. I have the most wonderful successful children even though I had to go to work. I felt I was more loving after coming back from work than while staying at home all time.

As a family, we had a wonderful three-week summer vacation. We visited several good friends and relatives in New Orleans, Pensacola, Miami, and, of course, Minnie and Mickey Mouse at Disney World. At this point in our lives, it was a blessing to be able to spend time together as a family.

In August of the same year, I was fortunate to join my daughter Deborah and her husband, Alex, for a fascinating trip to Bucharest, Romania, for the wedding of one of Alex's friends who both graduated from Harvard's Business School. Despite the enormous pain of the past years when my husband was fighting cancer, I feel blessed by the joy of my children, grandchildren, and by God. I have no words to express my gratitude for all the support I received: phone calls, letters, cards, e-mail, and prayers. It was a heavy-duty loss. Someone said, *"But I guess, some time he has to let life turn us upside-down. So we can learn how to live right side up."*

In thinking back, *my first episode* happened in December 1972 when a major earthquake destroyed a large portion of the capital city of Managua where I lived. We had just moved into our brand-new home and, with much sorrow, had to abandon it to move into a safer area. I was so attached to that new house that I suffered greatly because I had to leave it instead of being happy that all my family had been spared from certain death. I learned to identify my spiritual enemies; in this case, it was materialism. This particular experience taught me that I must not become attached to material things. I must trust in God and accept the circumstance he creates to keep me from harm or uses in teaching me valuable lessons.

My second episode happened when I experienced death after the earthquake.

My third episode that tested my conviction took place in 1979 when I fled my country on a three-week vacation because of its unstable political situation. I recognize that there are different interpretations toward the political situation in Central America. Many are fighting to free Central America from communism; others are fighting against the intervention of foreign countries. But my primary personal point of view is that as a responsible mother, my family comes first, and my first priority was to leave the country for the safety of my family. I do not think I was taking the easy road because I needed a great deal of courage to leave behind all I had worked for in my life to start all over again. Honestly, I was hoping that my departure was going to be for a short term and that eventually things will go back to normal. We left behind all our material belongings. We were supposed to go back, but instead, we stayed with our children in a safe place where we could begin a new life.

My fourth episode took place in 2000 when I lost my husband due to cancer.

This vacation has worn me down. The adversities I have gone through in my life have given me an opportunity to see my frail human weaknesses that God wants to turn into strengths. Each day is a growing experience. My faith and strength are based on a rock named Jesus.

I now realize that my three-week vacation that started in 1979 and became a long-term stay in this land has not been a waste of time after all. The succession of events has led me from one milestone toward another milestone that has enlightened my life. Moving to a new land; giving birth to my fifth daughter, Lilette Jill; getting a job at Chevron that started going just to get an employment application and ending working for so many years for this fantastic and huge oil company; attending a reputable university, the University of San Francisco (USF), and obtaining a bachelor of science degree and a master of science degree; becoming a University of California Berkeley Mom where all five of my daughters attended; I'm now fluent in English; and last but not least, even though sad, my companion passed away while *still on vacation.*

The political situation in Nicaragua brought my children on a vacation that has lasted over three decades. Coming on vacation to the U.S. and having to stay represented an uncertain future in a foreign country. But when I start counting my blessings, I firmly believe it was a great decision. I am a Nicaraguan with American citizenship. I am currently enjoying my grandchildren, in contact with good friends of my youth, traveling, playing the piano, involved at church by helping in the nursery, teaching Spanish to adults as a volunteer at the community center in my town, supporting a foundation in

Nicaragua, uploading videos to my YouTube channel on behalf of Nicaragua, and traveling domestic and around the world. All these activities keep me busy. What more can I ask? I am so grateful for my good fortune.

My family has been together even though one member of this clan went to heaven during our journey. I've heard so many times that together you'll be stronger. Even though the partner of my life left too soon in his life, I continued walking on this journey with five incredible daughters, four sons-in-law, and eleven grandchildren.

In retrospect, I have lived through extraordinary situations, and all the many lessons I've learned through so many experiences are priceless. When I feel I cannot handle a difficult situation, and I go through discouragement, weariness, indecision, and inertia, I remember how fortunate I am to be able to say that although I have gone through undesirable experiences, they did not destroy me. But rather, they have given me the self-confidence to realize that I can survive adversity and that I have priceless good fortune in marriage, children, health, and friends.

This journey has been a life-changing event. I give thanks for today, the present. My blessed life in this country has been a miracle and a humbling experience. If I had my life to live again, I wouldn't change anything. I will totally live it again. We rose from scratch! ¡Sí, se puede! Yes, you can!

To those moving to the U.S., keep the faith. You are true dreamers, and you must believe dreams come true. Keep dreaming! There is always a lesson to learn as well as a blessing to gain. You might have to go through injustice, but don't worry, it's just temporary. Don't look backward but instead, keep looking forward. God has good things up ahead of you.

Through this book, I am articulating my love by sharing my life with my children, grandchildren, and great-grandchildren who eventually will come and in particular to those moving into the U.S. Immigrants are not the enemies. They, in fact, are running away from the enemy that is oppressing them. They are looking for a place where they can grow, flourish, and rest. All they want is to protect their children and be able to enjoy peace. Their only desire is to build a house and a home. They are doing what our first settlers did and many of us have done. How can we forget that the majority of us are immigrants, or descendants of immigrants? These human beings are coming with hope and with a dream. Can we open our gates so that their dreams won't be simply a dream? I believe we need to secure our country but not with a five-billion wall. Security is essential at homes and in our nation, but let's look at the future. Let's implement a twenty-first century security. When I hear, "Build the wall!" I cannot help but hear instead, "Crucify him (them)!" (Mark 15:12–14).

I must say:

> *Who am I, sovereign Lord, and what is my*
> *family, that you have brought me this far?*
> —2 Samuel 7:18

*My legacy is: I worked as hard as I could
to protect my family and meet my goals.*

*I invite you to visit my channel:
Ilean Baltodano
YouTube*

Acknowledgments

Writing this memoir was something I have prayed for fervently. I would like to thank God for his mercy, and countless blessings in my life.

I would also like to thank, and I am forever indebted to Charlotte Somarriba, John F. Hughes, and Ofelia Gallo who wrote the foreword for this book. Thank you for your support, continued influence, and friendship. Thank you for all you've done to shape my life, either professionally or personally.

Also, thank you to my five daughters: Ilean, Claudia, Deborah, Kattya, and Lilette. I thank you for your support, and inspiration to me. We brought you to this country without giving you a choice, and you have accomplished and succeeded beyond any and all expectations.

In writing this book, I sought inspiration in those that seek freedom and safety, as I did in my journey, and I share this with the thousands of people who dare to take this treacherous journey.

Finally, this book is dedicated to the memory of my late husband, Francisco, who always supported my dreams and goals.

Addendum

Still on Vacation
In the middle of a pandemic

*T*hough many years have passed, I came to the United States while still young; married to a good man, who went to heaven too soon, and with five precious daughters who are my treasure. Now, on this long journey full of happy times and bad times, I find myself in the autumn of my life; a widow, with grandchildren; but, with the energy to speak up because if I don't the stones will do it for me.

There are times of peace and unfortunately, there are times of pandemic and hunger. The year 2020 will go down in history and we, including the whole world, are part of this incredible story. I hope that order, tranquility and happiness will come soon as the suffering that most people are experiencing is indescribable.

The country must unite to combat the pandemic and the political situation; united makes us stronger. Our country's leaders need a lot of wisdom to solve so many socio-political and socio-economic problems surrounding every State in the country. We, the people of the United States, are stoic, successful, and do not give up. Yes, we shed tears! Yes, we fall down! But, we always get up; we shake up our feathers and ascend like the Phoenix bird that arises from its own ashes.

Let's pray to God for a more orderly government and that this pestilence will soon go away. We can't give up hope!

The White House

The Madness of the Giant Goliath in the White House

Ilean Baltodano
2020

In life, we confront giants.
Many times, giants are not always
what they seem to be
and its powerful, fearful appearance
is not what we see.
We have a giant goliath
in the White House.
Metaphorically,
this giant has a height,
a figure which
forces him to walk with no balance.
He communicates illogically with no filter; and,
he portrays an offensive
and embarrassing ego,
a grandiose narcissism.
This blind ego
is making him vulnerable.
I love this country
which is great but not perfect, and
it is my adopted country.
This country needs a successor with
character, integrity, moral fiber, honesty,
and many more synonyms of character
this serving president
doesn't have.
Heaven will send us DAVID
to defeat GOLIATH

COVID-19

America's Dilemma: Saving Lives Vs. Saving the Economy

*T*he sad reality is that America and the world is at war with COVID-19. To win any war, an army with effective weapons is crucial. Is America ready to win this war? Let's stop blaming. The damage as to how this pandemic should have been handled is already done. Too many people have died in the most powerful country in the world. Now, let's fight this war with the right kinds of weapons, with strategy, and with tactic.

While we are hiding from COVID-19, we are disrupting the economy. Throughout our history, pandemics are not new. The economy has been disrupted in the past and the country has recovered with stoicism. The world is more technically, scientifically, and industrially advanced and that is an advantage if we compare this pandemic with the ones in the past.

Some people are getting restless. It feels like authorities are taking away our freedom; but, in reality, COVID-19 is the culprit. The Coronavirus is the felon. This virus is the real illegal alien controlling us.

While we are hiding, we are making the enemy weaker and eventually we will destroy it.

Nevertheless, let's be understanding to those who want to go out freely; the first amendment allows this, and also let's be sensitive to those who don't agree. Both have their own line of reasoning as long as they don't intimidate or endanger people's lives. Let's agree to disagree. Life isn't fair, but is still good.

Let's concentrate in attacking this enemy. This virus has deeply impacted too many families. I must say, ***Many Thanks! ¡Gracias!*** to the essential workers who are endangering their lives every day.

Saving Lives vs. Saving the Economy, this is a true dilemma. Let's keep the faith and also let's give a chance to the experts.

Let's pray for America's health to be restored in order to move to the next level.

Social Distancing

*C*hallenges and adversities will always come and we are all facing a major challenge. The COVID-19 situation is changing you, me and the whole world. Even though we are all different, from a global angle, we are all the same. There is just one human race. This is the time to unite. We need each other, together in faith, praising God.

We are all thirsty of love and encouragement. It's part of our human nature. Together, we are stronger; especially during this time of enforced social distancing. Let's verbalize our feelings over the phone, text or email. Even simple words are powerful. We can make someone happy. And, let's ask God to join us. He will deliver us from this major storm. God is our help. We don't know when this will change. But, we will pass this test with God's power. Let's walk by faith. This virus is becoming the equalizer. We are all in this together.

He will vindicate us but we have to invite Him. And, we might as well relax, because He can do the impossible.

The Control is Among Us

*H*ow are we going to control this virus? For now, the control is in our hands with well washed hands. Furthermore, just as this popular Spanish song entitled: *"With you in the distance" ["Contigo en la Distancia"]* the control is among us. And, last but not least, it is crucial we wear a mask and sometimes double masks to protect ourselves and others.

We have to admit, this virus is teaching us many lessons. The environment and the world are changing — fewer cars are circulating and consequently fewer accidents, and the environment is cleaner.

This virus is making us more humble. There is more love and compassion in our hearts. Now we know what it is like to be locked in a cage. Like those immigrant children.

Kids don't understand why grandma can't hug them. But, because of this virus, many children are enjoying more time with their parents.

This pandemic has made it clear we all need medical health care. Many have lost their jobs. Many are alone locked up. This is the time to use the technology for a good cause.

Power, money, and work are not, at this moment, a priority. Our health and the health of others are paramount. Yes, there is fear and it's normal.

We will return to the world again; but, let's not forget the environment. Let's treat our mother earth with love.

This is not political. Yes, we are going to defeat this virus with the help of God — our heavenly father.

The Betrayal–
Wednesday,
January 6, 2021

Words of a President
have
Consequences

We cannot erase the year 2020. We cannot erase January 6, 2021 betrayal while President Trump was trying to change the outcome of the election. This day was one of the darkest days causing five dead.

Riots have happened and will continue happening. They are characterized as violent public disturbances against authority, property, or people. But, there is no excuse for what happened in January 6, 2021.

The years 2020 and 2021 are not ordinary epochs; but, these are times to pledge to righteousness and loyalty to our country – America the beautiful.

Words of a president have consequences. They can either inspire or become dangerous and inflammatory and that was the sad situation in January 6, 2021, the darkest day in the history of a president who misled U.S. citizens rather than accept defeat.

"Those who can make you believe absurdities,
Can make you commit atrocities."
Voltaire

A new chapter

Change of Command
Wednesday, January 20, 2021

*I*n spite of the events on Wednesday, January 20, 2021 the country is moving towards a new chapter in the history of the United States of America with hopefulness and faith.

The first female vice president; and, the first woman vice president of color is a historical episode.

> **"I may be the first, but won't be the last."**
> Kamala Harris
>
> Words during her first speech as Vice President
> of the United States of America.

Let's hope Biden/Harris will make a change. As I mentioned earlier, let's pray to God for a more orderly government and that this epidemic will soon go away. We can't give up hope!

In Memoriam

We'll always
Remember
Them

*T*he world has lost too many precious lives. Although they are no longer physically with us, their spirits are with us. They won't come back. But eventually, we'll go to them. The get together will be amazing!

I present my condolences to the families of those already gone to heaven. Let's move on, even though the pain is huge.

Let's light a candle for them!

About the Author

Ilean Baltodano is of Hispanic / Latin American ethnic origin. She came to the United States of America in 1979 for a three-week vacation and, due to political unrest and conflict, along with her husband and children, did not return to Nicaragua even though it was a very difficult decision because they left everything behind and had to start from scratch.

Ilean seeks a purpose for her life. After her retirement from Chevron, she continues staying busy: having fun with her grandchildren; playing the piano; teaching Spanish to adults as a volunteer in a community center; and supporting a foundation in Nicaragua called *Asociación y Colegio Pan y Amor*, a nonprofit organization that educates, feeds, and provides support and job training for disadvantaged children. She enjoys walking two to three miles every other day and listening to audio books. She travels domestic and around the world. She enjoys traveling because it gives her a vast education into new cultures, religion, history, food, and specially people. It teaches her to have an open mind to love people from different places and reminds her that we are all human beings. Even though she is in the autumn of her life, she has the energy to speak up on behalf of Nicaragua via her channel on YouTube: Ilean Baltodano.

She has a pragmatic way of looking at life. Ilean, Francisco, and daughters were all holding hands along their journey of trials and blessings in a foreign country, but suddenly, Francisco let go and went to heaven way too soon. Ilean went through a painful experience when she lost her husband. In the middle of this experience, Ilean had the confidence that eventually everything will work out as a single mother. She lives in Northern California.

Starting this book was easy for her but finishing this memoir was really hard. She was able to finish writing this portion of her life with God's help and the support and encouragement of her daughters.